Brockway Mountain Stories
The History of Brockway Mountain Drive and Keweenaw Mountain Lodge

Mudminnow Press, LLC
P.O. Box 36
Copper Harbor, Michigan 49918

Copyright @ 2023 Mudminnow Press, LLC
All rights reserved, including the right of reproduction in whole
or in part in any form or technology.

Written by Paul LaVanway
Cover and interior design by Smythtype Design

Printed in the United States
10 9 8 7 6 5 4 3 2 1

Mudminnow Press First Edition, 2023

ISBN 978-0-9833018-0-6

Brockway Mountain Stories
The History of Brockway Mountain Drive and Keweenaw Mountain Lodge

by Paul LaVanway

Mudminnow Press
Copper Harbor, Michigan

INTRODUCTION

"History doesn't repeat itself, but it rhymes" —attributed to Mark Twain

The Brockway Mountain Drive Story and the Keweenaw Mountain Lodge Story sprang to life almost two decades ago as a series of articles for the Keweenaw County Historical Society's quarterly publication, *The Superior Signal*. At the time, the objective was to document these Depression-era work relief projects, providing a clearer understanding of the Great Depression and its impact upon the local area.

Enduring reader interest in Keweenaw history and the tale of how these two legacy programs came about—the building of Brockway Mountain Drive and the construction of "the Lodge"—soon resulted in the formal publication of separate booklets telling "the Story" of each of these projects.

These dual publications, out of print and unavailable for a number of years, are now back in print by way of this 'combined publication.'

Historical accounts, of course, are the result of the time in which they are written and are subject to revision. This is especially true for the Brockway Mountain Drive and Keweenaw Mountain Lodge narratives. As that timeless proverb reminds us, "the only constant is change."

Accordingly, an update is appropriate:

Changes Up On Brockway—The Summit:

The key change occurring up on Brockway following publication of the Brockway Mountain Drive Story commenced with the decision of Clyde and Lloyd Wescoat to relinquish their family's nearly 80 year ownership of the 320 acres which comprised Brockway's summit—"the top of Brockway."

Wanting to ensure that the public could continue to enjoy access to this scenic and recreational landmark, while protecting the land and natural environment from development, the Wescoats worked in collaboration with a variety of nature and community-minded organizations to achieve an agreement for sale of the property.

Purchased by Eagle Harbor Township on February 14, 2013, the parcel was paid for through a $498,000 Michigan Natural Resources Trust Fund grant, with the balance of the $650,000 purchase price coming from matching donations from Eagle Harbor Township, The Nature Conservancy, Houghton Keweenaw Conservation District, Keweenaw Land Trust, Copper Country Audubon Society, as well as from hundreds of individual contributors.

Michigan Governor Rick Snyder's comments at the Tuesday, August 13, 2013, Brockway Summit dedication and ribbon-cutting ceremony were poignant: "This is of great benefit to both current and future generations...not only because it is a special place, but because special people made it happen and it shows what can happen when people work together...what an incredible win for all of us."

Changes Up On Brockway—The Overlook:

September of 2012 saw the completion of a major upgrade to the Keweenaw County Road Commission's Brockway Overlook roadside park, which provides a commanding view of Lake Superior, the Village of Copper Harbor, Lake Fanny Hooe, and the eastern ridgeline of the Keweenaw Peninsula.

Planning for the improved lookout stretched back almost a decade, with project work encompassing three components, including property acquisition, interpretive signage and construction of a two-tiered walkway and viewing area. Restoration and extension of the promontory's rock walls was included as part of the plan.

Cost of the construction portion of the project was approximately a half million dollars, with funding provided by the Michigan Department of Transportation, the Federal Highway Administration, and the Keweenaw County Road Commission. The construction portion of the design was completed by Bacco Construction of Iron Mountain; the interpretive signage was provided by Conservation By Design of Silver City, NM.

The roadside park was dedicated to early Copper Harbor residents and tourism entrepreneurs, Harold and Serene Wescoat. The Wescoat family contributed 20 percent toward the property purchase.

The Lodge—A Return to Private Ownership:

The 2006–07 $3.3 million expansion of the Keweenaw Mountain Lodge principally entailed the addition of a 6,000 square foot conference center, including winterization of the main clubhouse, the six room motel unit, and 13 of the 24 rental cabins.

Financed by a $1.754 million U.S. Economic Development Administration grant and a $1.273 million USDA Rural Development loan, the terms of the financing generally required that the facility be operated year-round, towards providing additional yearlong employment opportunities. Of note, debt service repayment projections for the expanded facility were based upon an increase in both revenue and income, the same accruing from year-round operation of the resort.

Regrettably, despite several years of year-round operation, the Lodge business consistently failed to achieve the revenue and profit targets which had been provided for in the expansion financial plan. Rather, winter operation of the facility generated substantial seasonal losses, with the KML operation, in aggregate, being unable to generate the funds necessary to service the incurred debt. In response, the Keweenaw County Board of Commissioners decided on August 17, 2011, that effective with the upcoming 2011–12 winter season, the Lodge would cease winter operations. The resort thus returned to its traditional mid-May to mid-October operating schedule.

Over the next several years meetings and discussions were held between County and Federal officials, with Keweenaw County aiming to eliminate, if not at least reduce, the debt repayment provisions associated with the Federal loan and grant. From the County's perspective, these discussions proved to be unproductive.

Concurrently, the County Board and the Park Board of Trustees initiated a variety of management and operational program changes, towards achieving a reduction in Lodge operating costs and/or an increase in revenues and income. Lamentably, these efforts neither translated into a permanent improvement in the resort's profitability nor in the ability of the operation to service the debt taken-on to finance the 2006–07 expansion and winterization.

The non-repayment of the Federal debt reached a turning point in July of 2017, with USDA Rural Development (RDA) and U.S. Economic Development (EDA) reaching an agreement with Keweenaw County by which the Keweenaw Mountain Lodge would be listed for sale with the net proceeds of the sale being distributed 50.83% to RDA and 49.17% to EDA. While Keweenaw County would receive none of the proceeds of the KML sale, its debt to the two Federal agencies would be eliminated.

Listed for sale at $1.5 million later that summer, Keweenaw County received several offers to purchase the property. The first such offer, made in late September of 2017, was from Anthony Lane Partners LLC of Dallas, Texas; although the non-binding offer was accepted by the Keweenaw County Board, Anthony Lane Partners subsequently opted to terminate its bid. A second offer to purchase was received from Adoba Hotels, however, similar to the Anthony Lane Partners situation, while the Adoba offer to purchase was accepted by the Keweenaw County Board, Adoba subsequently chose to withdraw. No other credible offers to purchase the KML property were received. The resort remained unsold for the balance of 2017.

As 2018 began and the Keweenaw Mountain Lodge remained unsold, the decision was made to sell the property by auction. The Maas Companies of Rochester, Minnesota was retained to market and conduct a public auction to liquidate the resort. Included in the sale of the 177 acre parcel was the historic clubhouse and conference center, two liquor licenses plus commercial bar and kitchen facilities, the 9-hole golf course and tennis court, all of the rental cabins and motel units, plus applicable support equipment, furnishings and personal property.

The live sit-down public auction of the property was held in the Keweenaw Mountain Lodge's Conference Center and began at 10 a.m. on Thursday, July 26, 2018. Before the morning was over, the resort was sold, ending 84 years of (sometimes intermittent) Keweenaw County ownership. The auction was won by John Lamb of 4 Lambs Properties, Corpus Christi, Texas, with a high bid of $1.175 million. With the addition of a 10% buyer premium, the total cost of the property came in at $1.292.5 million.

Ironically, this was not the end of the story regarding the sale of the Keweenaw Mountain Lodge for, within a matter of days, John Lamb came to feel that bidding as high as he did to purchase the resort was, on his part, too much of an "impulsive…spur-of-the-moment decision." Shortly thereafter, Lamb worked out an agreement wherein he reassigned his interest in the KML purchase agreement to the second-highest bidder, John Mueller of Austin, Texas.

John Mueller closed on the purchase on September 5, 2018, with he and his wife, Widad, operating the resort under the auspices of the legal entity, Keweenaw Resort, LLC.

Today's "Lodge" retains its classic historic character, while promoting nature-based tourism and outdoor experiences. In 2022, the resort acquired a neighboring 380 acres from Keweenaw County, bringing its total holdings to nearly 560 acres. In so doing, the resort had created additional opportunities for visitors to experience the Keweenaw wilderness.

Brockway Mountain Drive Story

West Bluff — Brockway Mountain Drive

Running up the spine of the Keweenaw's West Bluff, Brockway Mountain Drive features spectacular panoramic views of Lake Superior and breathtaking vistas of the surrounding wilderness. The highest scenic roadway between the Alleghenies and the foothills of the Rockies, the route is a favorite of tourists and visitors alike. During the fall color season especially, the road is a "must see." It is regularly recognized as the best scenic drive in Michigan, if not all of the Midwest.

Few landmarks symbolize the Keweenaw's history and natural wonders more powerfully than the mountain drive. Indeed, the road has come to epitomize the best the Copper Country has to offer.

Amidst these accolades, what is ironic is that while it has been 75 years since the road was first opened to the public, the Brockway Mountain Drive story has never been fully told. The history of the road, as well its most basic facts, is largely unknown.

PRELUDE TO THE ROAD

The possibility of constructing a scenic drive along the ridgeline of the Keweenaw Peninsula was first proposed by Warren H. Manning, a nationally known landscape architect and engineer.

An avid proponent of the conservation of America's lands and wilderness, Manning came to the Copper Country in the early 1920s, having been retained to design Calumet's Agassiz Park. It was at that time, while on a trip through this most northern part of Michigan, that Manning proposed a scenic highway to run on the summit of the range of the Keweenaw.

Photo of nationally known landscape engineer and architect, Warren H. Manning, (b. 1860-d.1938). Manning was the first proponent of constructing a scenic drive along the ridgeline of the Keweenaw. *Credit: Wikipedia*

It would take the start of the 1930s and the beginning of the Great Depression for interest to be sparked in pursuing the idea of a summit road. The economic collapse proved devastating to the Keweenaw. Hardship was widespread, with many not only loosing their jobs, but also their savings and homes. With but one industry—copper mining—as its dominant employer, the Keweenaw was hard hit, with the early 1930s finding two-thirds of the area's workforce unemployed.

Against this backdrop, it was local and state governments that stepped forward with relief measures designed to alleviate suffering and enable the population to maintain at least some minimal standard of living. Federal efforts to provide work for the unemployed were mired in a quagmire of political and legislative wrangling.

The Keweenaw County Road Commission (KCRC) took the lead in providing work to those who were employable and who had registered on local relief rolls. The Road Commission—an organization which throughout most of the 1920s had a workforce ranging between 70–80 individuals—suddenly found itself the employer of upwards of 600 and 700 men.

THE DEVELOPMENT OF A PLAN

The summer of 1932 found the Road Commission grappling with the issue of developing economically feasible, yet worthwhile, work relief projects. Opportunities were sought which would help broaden the Keweenaw's economic base, especially, undertakings which would help jump-start the Copper Country's fledgling tourism industry. Amidst these conditions, William Manning's earlier proposal for a highway running up the crest of the Keweenaw was revisited.

What resulted from initial planning were proposals for not one, but rather, two road projects: Lakeshore Drive, what is now M-26 between Eagle Harbor and Copper Harbor, and Brockway Mountain Drive, which was designed as an offshoot of Lakeshore Drive.

Relative to construction of the summit road—what would later become Brockway Mountain Drive—the Road Commission considered three different alternatives before selecting the final route.

The first proposal was for a road that would follow the existing route of Brockway Mountain Drive, running from its Silver River end up to the top of the West Bluff. Ending at the top of the scenic overlook, the road would have gone no farther. Traffic would then need to turn around and descend the summit the same way it went up. A "least cost" option, this alternative followed (on its western end) what was the preexisting route of the original Military Road for the first $2^2/_3$ miles of its five mile length.

The second alternative included the route outlined in option one, above. However, in lieu of the road ending at the top of the scenic overlook, this scheme featured the road continuing to run toward the east, following the course of the West Bluff ridgeline, prior to descending to rejoin Lakeshore Drive near Copper Harbor. This option is what today most would recognize as the nine mile long route of contemporary Brockway Mountain Drive.

Lastly, there was a third option. This alternative contemplated a summit road which followed the existing route of the mountain drive from Copper Harbor on up to the top of West Bluff. However, on its western descent from West Bluff, the road would have traversed to the southwest, cutting diagonally across Upson Creek Valley. It would have then run up and across the top of the summit of Mount Lookout (i.e., the ridgeline also known as Mount Baldy, located due south of Lake Bailey), before proceeding west, terminating at its junction with the Eagle Harbor Shortcut Road. Never built, this third prototype was the most expensive option. From an engineering point of view, at 16 miles in length, it would have been the most technically venturesome.

The Road Commission, out of the three plans that had been offered up for consideration, selected the second option, the nine mile long "middle" alternative. This was a joint decision made by the three members of the Commission—Chairman William F. Hartman, Member Ocha Potter, and Member William R. Bolley—with the support and concurrence of longtime KCRC Engineer, William C. "Clem" Veale.

Late 1932 found the Road Commission implementing actions across a variety of fronts, all designed to prepare for the start of construction the following spring.

Clearing of trees, on left, along the western end of Brockway Mountain Drive, 1933. Note that path of the earlier Military Road is visible in center foreground of photograph. *Credit: Clyde Wescoat Collection*

Most notably, to pay for the road, KCRC obtained funding from the Reconstruction Finance Corporation (RFC). A federal agency established during the Herbert Hoover Administration, RFC played a major roll in helping to fund relief programs, initiatives which in subsequent years would be taken over by the New Deal. In addition, the Road Commission initiated talks that led to the Michigan State Highway Department assuming financial and operational responsibility for construction of the Lakeshore Drive project. As reflected in the Road Commission's official minutes:

Minutes of November 14, 1932:
- State to take over construction of Eagle Harbor to Copper Harbor Highway program. Calumet and Hecla Consolidated Copper Company, through President MacNaughton, donates park land on Lake Bailey to assist in the state take-over of project; offer is conditioned upon the state take-over of the highway.
- Reconstruction Finance Corporation loan to KCRC for $30,000–$35,000 through State Highway Commission.

Minutes of December 9, 1932:
- Stop all road work except snowplowing to build-up treasury for spring construction.
- Implement pay reductions and layoffs.

CONSTRUCTION OF THE ROAD

Construction of the mountain drive started in the spring of 1933. Remarkably, the basic road was completed and opened for traffic in October, less than four months from start to finish.

On average, 150–200 men were employed on the project. Early October, 1933, however, found a crew of 300 working on the road. This temporary increase in the manning level probably reflected a decision to try and finish-up the project, to attempt to get the summit highway open—despite its relatively crude and rudimentary condition—before the end of the tourist season and the start of winter.

Pay for workmen was $0.25 per hour, with each man earning, on average, $36.00 a month. (As an aside, the $36 per month figure would be adjusted upward in the later years of the depression, first to $40, and later, to $44. Work hours were also adjusted by the amount needed by each man to house, feed, and clothe his family. Thus, a man with a large family was provided with more hours of work than a man whose family was small.)

One of the better descriptions of the construction effort was related by John W. Jackson in an interview contained in the June 7, 1986, edition of the *Daily Mining Gazette*. Jackson, who had

Photograph of the western section of Brockway Mountain Drive, as one heads from the Silver River entrance of the road towards the top of West Bluff. Along this stretch, the highway follows the original route of the Military Road; the route is similar to a forest road and is characterized by a gradual ascent and the relative absence of solid rock. Probably late 1930s / early 1940s. *Credit: Paul LaVanway Collection*

Employee ID badge - Keweenaw County Road Commission. Workers had to show this type of tag in order to record their work hours, receive their pay, etc. From 1930s. *Credit: Paul LaVanway Collection*

Winter view from western end of Mountain Drive. Lake Bailey visible in distance. Probably winter, 1933-1934. *Credit: Keenwaw County Historical Society Collection*

served as Keweenaw County Road Commission Engineer from 1963 until his retirement in 1971, had worked on the Brockway construction project as the KCRC's principal on-site engineer. In looking back, Jackson said:

"It was all hand work. We had to put a bunch of men to work on a meaningful project and that was the job.

"The months were short, sometimes only 10 days. We alternated crews so that each man would get in his time. I guess that is where someone came up with the figure of 300 men being used on the job. I seem to recall less than that, but then, that was almost 50 years ago."

Jackson remembered best the grades and the elevations. "There was never a survey instrument used to level the road grades. It was all done by eye. It was an interesting accomplishment. Locating the run of the road over that conglomerate ridge was simply looking for a level place to put the road, and placing the grades ahead of the gang of men."

Jackson went on to say, "the grading of Brockway was all manual, except for Charley Maki's team of horses from Copper Harbor, who hauled dirt for the grades. To help keep the grade of the road level, most of the fill for the road came from the ditches along the side of the road, all hand dug."

"Those were the stipulations that the job called for, no machines. It was a unique road, too, one with a view of the lake on one side, and the valley on the other. We were asked to come up with jobs for the men. And that was it."

Further to the commentary contained in Jackson's interview, longtime Copper Harbor summer resident Stan Martin reminisced: "I clearly recall Charley Maki's team of horses being used up on Brockway. I'd see them head up the hill each morning, only it wasn't Charley running the team—no, Charley was out fishing—it was Charley's son, Wesley—Wesley Maki. Wesley took the team up the hill each morning—he ran the team. Wesley couldn't have been much more than 16, maybe 17, years old at the time." As an entertaining side note, it was Charley Maki's grandson, Glenn "Sonny" Stevens, who identified the horses used up on Brockway: "...they were named "Nick" and "Dick"—when I was a kid, Jim Wescoat drilled that into my head."

View from western end of the mountain drive. Lake Bailey and Mount Lookout (Mt. Baldy) visible in distance. Note presence of round, "ball bearing," gravel in foreground. About 1933-1934. *Credit: Paul LaVanway Collection*

View of West Bluff just east of the Military Road turn-off. From the image, it appears that the route is primarily being used as a single lane dirt road. Probably mid to late 1930s. *Credit: Paul LaVanway Collection*

Additional insights on the mountain drive construction project were offered by Bill Clark, of Clark Point at Great Sand Bay. Clark grew up in Copper Falls, living in what had been the Copper Falls Mining Company's "Agent's House." Clark vividly remembered trucks traveling through Copper Falls each morning—and returning every evening—as they traveled the Eagle Harbor Shortcut Road:

> "We only lived 100 feet off the highway and the men working up on Brockway went right by our house. They'd pick the men up down in Mohawk, down in Ahmeek and places like that, and haul them out to the worksite in the back of dump trucks. They'd set up seats, made out of boards, in the back of the trucks so that the men would have a place to sit down; that way, they could carry a dozen, maybe 15, men in a truck. It beat walking or riding a horse and buggy, but not by much. If it was raining or especially as the weather started to get cold, it's a wonder they had the energy left to do any work."

Clark recollected that his father, Wesley Clark, who had been laid-off as a Mining Engineer from Calumet & Hecla in 1931, was able to get "hired on" as an Engineer on the mountain drive construction project.

> "Dad usually worked with Harry Swanson—he was one of the Engineers from the Road Commission—Swanson worked as one of the surveyors up on the job. Dad always said that what was unique about the job was that they surveyed the road after it was built, not before. Evidently, that was not the way it was supposed to be done. Dad was just amazed by the mathematics that went into measuring and calculating the turns and curves up there; he talked about that for years afterwards."

Lastly, Clark recalled his Dad mentioning a controversial issue that had arisen up on the mountain drive worksite:

> "Ocha Potter's (one of the KCRC Commissioners) college-aged son came home from traveling overseas, and he (i.e., Potter) had him put to work—put him on the payroll up on the mountain drive job. Normally, that wouldn't be an issue, but times were tough. The Road Commission

Approaching West Bluff from the Silver River end of the mountain drive. Late 1930s. *Credit: Paul LaVanway Collection*

Heading to the top of West Bluff from the Silver River end of the mountain drive, late 1940s. This photograph taken in almost the same location as the photograph opposite—just east of the turn-off to old Military Road. Note growth of vegetation since mid-late 1930s. *Credit: Paul LaVanway Collection*

was limiting the number of hours and pay that even the married men—the men with families and kids to feed—could earn. There was a real undercurrent of dissention over Potter's kid being up there, but most of the workers were hesitant to say anything. Ocha Potter was the man from the Road Commission who was in control of nearly every employees pay rate and the number of hours they could work. It wasn't a good situation. However, probably fortunately, because of the nature of the work—he (i.e., Potter's son) didn't last too long."

Several field notes and records still survive from the scenic road construction project. These documents indicate that the majority of the work went into construction of the eastern leg of the highway, that is, the West Bluff to Copper Harbor corridor.

Construction on the western section of the highway, from the Silver River "end" on up to the top of West Bluff, with its more gradual ascent and relative absence of solid rock, was simpler. It was not dissimilar to what might have been encountered in the course of building any other Keweenaw County highway. In contrast, building the road across the top of the eastern end of the ridgeline, with its steep ascents and declines, amid sheer cliffs and precipitous escarpments, was a challenging and potentially dangerous task.

Archival records and notes chronicle that the workers and engineers—probably similar to workers the world over—attached names and labels to many of the areas and features they worked on. These identifications and sobriquets spanned the eastern leg of the road, from the top of West Bluff on down to the bottom: East Valley, East Hill, Beaver Dam Overlook, West Cracked Rock, Cracked Rock, Birch Valley, Kettle Gulch, Hartman's View, Big Curve and Brockway's View.

Another view of the approach to the top of West Bluff. Late 1930s. *Credit: Paul LaVanway Collection*

William C. "Clem" Veale, on right, pictured with Michigan State Highway Commissioner Howard Hill, on left. Late 1950s. Veale served as Engineer of the Keweenaw County Road Commission from 1922 to 1963. *Credit: Keweenaw County Road Commision*

THE ROAD OPENS

By early October, 1933, area motorists, out exploring while driving around the Copper Country, found that work on the mountain drive had advanced to the point where the road was passable. And, much like motorists everywhere, they started to use it.

Excerpts contained in the Tuesday, October 10, 1933, edition of the *Daily Mining Gazette* reported:

> "Work on the scenic drive between Eagle Harbor and Copper Harbor, which is being constructed under the direction of the Keweenaw County Road Commission, is progressing rapidy.... Rough grading is now being completed.... Several automobiles went over this stretch this weekend, but motorists are cautioned against using the road until grading and surfacing has been completed.... About 300 men are now employed on the drive. Since unnecessary traffic interferes with the work being done, motorists are asked to refrain from using any part of the road until after 3 o'clock daily, except Saturday and Sunday. The road will be open for general traffic from Saturday noon until Monday morning."

Brockway Mountain Drive was "officially" opened for the first time on Saturday, October 14, 1933. The same day, the *Daily Mining Gazette* advised their readers to enter the drive from the Eagle Harbor end, noting that, "difficulty will be encountered only if it rains, which will make the going difficult in some places."

The week of October 22, 1933, the Road Commission announced that the name of the road would be Brockway Mountain Drive, bearing the name of respected

The photo above, dated July 7, 1934, shows a work party grading the road on the east end of Brockway Mountain Drive overlooking Copper Harbor and Lake Fanny Hooe.
Credit: Keweenaw County Historical Society Collection

and beloved pioneer settler, Daniel D. Brockway. Interestingly, the Road Commission's decision to name the highway after Brockway came on the heels of several entreaties from one of the then owners of the top of the summit, Alfred W. Blom. On several different occasions Blom had corresponded with KCRC Engineer Clem Veale, requesting that the top of the summit be named "Blom Mountain," and the road, presumably, "Blom Mountain Drive."

In announcing its decision to name the road after Brockway, the Road Commission predicted that the opening of the scenic drive would mark a new stage in the development of the tourist industry in the Keweenaw; that it would be a main attraction which would help Copper Country businessmen build a profitable and successful tourist trade.

There was never a "grand opening" or "ribbon cutting" to formally mark the opening of the mountain drive. While a formal opening ceremony was proposed, to have coincided with the planned, June, 1934, opening of Lakeshore Drive, it never occurred.

Among the "grand opening" festivities discussed, however, were, "bringing up the Governor for the cutting of a ribbon that would be stretched out across the entrances of both of the roads—a Copper Harbor opening day pageant, to include, an attack on Fort Wilkins by Indians in costume and a defense by men in uniforms—floats with French Annie, Brockway, Bunyan, and copper miners—a banquet in the evening—and, fireworks on Brockway's Nose for 10,000 or more people in the valley below at Copper Harbor."

Amidst discussion of the various "opening and dedication" proposals, a delay developed in completing the Lakeshore Drive project, with the road not opening until October 12, 1934. Apparently, the idea of conducting a grand opening ceremony so "late in the season" (at that time, the "tourist season" ended right after Labor Day; mid-September, at the latest) was thought to be anticlimactic. As a result, plans for formal opening and dedication ceremonies were shelved. There is yet one more intriguing aspect to the story. Following the naming and opening of Brockway Mountain Drive, there then followed an effort to rename the top of the summit "Brockway's Bluff," or, alternatively, "Mt. Brockway." Apparently, the new name never completely "took." While a few contemporary maps label the top of the summit "Mt. Brockway," most, including all those

"East Hill" area, probably 1933–34. Photograph caption identifies the route as "Keweenaw Mountain Drive." Note lack of vegetation. Compare to photograph below.
Credit: Paul LaVanway Collection

"East Hill" area. Compare to earlier photograph, above. Probably about 1935–1936.
Credit: Paul LaVanway Collection

prepared by the U. S. Geological Survey—relying upon information from the U. S. Board on Geographic Names—designate the peak as "West Bluff." Accordingly, while users of the route are safe to assume that they are driving on Brockway Mountain Drive, the reality of the situation is that they may be scaling—"West Bluff," or, "Mount Brockway"—dependent upon which government agency provided the information for the map they are using.

WORK ON THE ROAD CONTINUES

Work on the mountain drive was suspended during the winter of 1933–34, resuming the following spring. Over the course of the winter, the Road Commission obtained funding under the Federal Emergency Relief Administration (FERA) and Civil Works Administration (CWA) programs, using plan monies to both start construction on the Keweenaw Mountain Lodge, as well as to complete work on the mountain drive.

The May 24, 1934, issue of *The Calumet News* announced the resumption of work on the mountain drive, noting that use of the road would temporarily be restricted to one-way traffic, and that it would only be open to the public on Sundays and holidays.

It was at this time that the first of the mountain drive's distinctive stone walls were built. The "rock guard rails," as they were known at the time, were 10' in length, and interconnected by 2' square rock piers. The walls were carefully constructed from cut and fitted fieldstone. The top of the walls and piers were covered with what a mason would call a "concrete wash."

Approximately 1,900 feet of this type of wall was built alongside the roadway. Interestingly, this "first type" of Brockway stone wall turned out to be nearly identical to another stone wall that had been completed the year before. This "other" stone wall was located along the famous "Going-To-The-Sun Road" in Glacier National Park in northwest Montana.

Photo of the eastern horizon of the Keweenaw Peninsula, taken from just below the southern side of West Bluff, probably early 1940s. Single, stand-alone, "rock guard rails," with "formed and poured concrete cap" at upper left in photo. "Beaver Dam" visible in photo at middle, right. Lake Fanny Hooe, East Bluff and golf course fairways of Keweenaw Mountain Lodge visible across top right of photo.
Credit: Paul LaVanway Collection

View of southeast corner of southern escarpment of West Bluff. Late 1930s.
Credit: Paul LaVanway Collection

Another early image of West Bluff, possibly taken from either the "West Cracked Rock" or "Cracked Rock" overlook area. Note "ball bearing" gravel in foreground of photograph, the gravel having been sourced from the Lake Superior shoreline. Probably about 1934. *Credit: MTU Archives & Copper County Historical Collections*

East view of the Mountain Drive as it exits Birch Valley. In the distance, it appears that the clubhouse of the Keweenaw Mountain Lodge is in the process of being constructed; accordingly, this photograph would likely date to summer, 1934.
Credit: Paul LaVanway Collection

View of West Bluff from "Beaver Dam" overlook. Notice road appears to be hard surfaced in this photograph. Probably early 1940s.
Credit: Paul LaVanway Collection

Much of the work performed in 1934 focused on smoothing out roadway curves, leveling elevations, and widening the road. Copper Harbor summer resident, Stan Martin, recalled driving the route right after it opened:

> "At first, it was just God awful. It was rough and full of ruts and potholes—just terrible to drive on."

Martin, who had been born in 1918, went on to say:

> "I was young and, at the time, just starting to drive—it seemed, though, that driving up on the mountain drive was just about continuous downshifting and braking and then reaccelerating. What really made it bad was, in order to save money, they went down to the shore of Superior and got beach stone and brought it up and used it as road gravel—well, it was just like driving on ball bearings—you'd put on the brakes and, if you were lucky, maybe you'd stop a hundred or two hundred feet later. As bad as it was at the beginning, though, within a year or two, it got A LOT better."

The improved condition of the road was reflected in gains in the popularity of the route. A road commission statistical study, conducted during the first half of July, 1934, tracked use of the road, both by state residents—many of whom were believed to be from points outside of the Copper Country—as well as by tourists from outside of the state. The data from the study indicated: "On July 1, 296 cars counted on the drive, 20 of them from other states. On July 4, the count was 266 and 21; on July 8, 225 and 29. On July 15, 320 Michigan cars and 42 from other states."

The condition of the road was sufficiently good that the Keweenaw Historical Society featured a trip over the scenic drive as a highlight of its July 25, 1934, society picnic. Members were encouraged to, "start at Eagle Harbor, taking that route to the top of the mountain, where a group picnic will be held at the lookout. Following a trip to Fort Wilkins, members can either travel back to Eagle Harbor by the "old road," or, take the scenic drive from Copper Harbor, as the highway is now open for two-way traffic. Afterwards, a white fish dinner will be served at the Lake Breeze Hotel at Eagle Harbor at 6:30."

"FINISHING" WORK

Work continued on the mountain drive the following year, 1935, however, this was mostly intermittent maintenance work, the highway being generally complete.

Keweenaw County Road Commission board minutes for June 14, 1935, reference the scenic roadway being finished, indicating that "....Brockway Mountain Drive has been built for less than $40,000..."

That fall, on November 30, 1935, the Road Commission held a "special meeting" to discuss "the new Works Progress Administration (WPA) program and its use in employing men."

WPA workers were employed on the mountain drive in 1936, with work focusing on smoothing the roadway (prior to the hard paving of the road surface, ruts and "washboarding" were ongoing problems). Then, in 1937, the mountain drive's stone walls were augmented, adding 660' of wall to the 1,918' of "rock guard rail" that was constructed in 1934.

This "second type" of stone wall or "rubble guard rail" was constructed in two general areas: 1) Up at the very top of West Bluff, and, 2) just above "Brockway's View," as an eastern extension to what had previously been the end of the "piered" wall. This later stone wall was constructed in single, stand alone, segments. A total of 66 separate sections, each one 10' in length, were built.

Adjacent and above "Brockway's View," the new walls were constructed out of a combination of "rubble stone" and poor rock; while up at the top of West Bluff, they were built primarily from of a dark gray, basalt, poor rock. Covered on the top with a "formed and poured concrete cap," these walls appear—at least in comparison to the earlier, cut and fitted fieldstone, "piered" walls—to be relatively crude.

While it may seem strange that some of the last stone walls constructed were located at the very top of the summit—where they were most needed—there is a plausible explanation. By 1934–35, the top of West Bluff was in the midst of being sold by its two out of area owners, Arthur Dakin and Alfred Blom, to

Lake Superior from top of West Bluff. Note smoke from coal fired steamship in distance.1933–1934
Credit: Paul LaVanway Collection

View of Lake Medora from southern escarpment of West Bluff.
Credit: Paul LaVanway Collection

Construction work on adjacent Lakeshore Drive, between the east entrance to Brockway Mountain Drive and "High Bridge." 1933. The Brockway Mountain Drive and Lakeshore Drive road construction projects were both begun at about the same time. The 14 mile-long Lakeshore Drive project was first proposed by long-time KCRC Engineer Wm. C. "Clem" Veale. It was built as a joint KCRC-Michigan State Highway Department Project and was paid for by the State Highway Department using funds from both the National Highway Recovery Program and the 1934 Hayden-Cartwright federal highway stabilization program. First opened to traffic on Friday, October 12, 1934, the total estimated construction cost of the Laskeshore Drive project was $56,573.
Credit: Keweenaw County Road Commision

View of Lakes Upson and Bailey from West Bluff summit. The roadway of Brockway Mountain Drive has not yet been constructed. 1933.
Credit: Paul LaVanway Collection

View of Lakes Upson and Bailey from atop the summit of West Bluff, likely from early 1940s. Compare to photograph above.
Credit: Clyde Wescoat Collection

Houghton residents Harold Wescoat and John Salmi. At the time, even though the West Bluff loop road had been constructed, there was no written easement agreement providing the Road Commission the legal right to use the property. Lengthy negotiations ensued; it was not until October 29, 1935—two years following construction of the road—that a right-of-way agreement between the parties was finalized. Apparently, the Road Commission decided to wait until the easement agreement was complete before constructing the "rock guard rails" across the West Bluff property.

The use of WPA workers on the mountain drive project was probably intermittent and of a relatively limited duration. By 1936, the construction of the mountain drive was at its culmination; it was basically a finished project.

Paradoxically, the building of the mountain drive is often—incorrectly—attributed to the WPA. Possibly this is because the WPA was the last of the "work relief" programs to be used to perform work on the highway. That said the WPA came on the scene long after the road was constructed. In fact, by the time the WPA appeared on the stage, the mountain drive was already open and in use. Clearly, the credit for the building of the mountain drive belongs not to the WPA, but rather, to the employees and Engineers of the Keweenaw County Road Commission.

TRANSITION AND EVOLUTION

The mountain drive was not hard surfaced until the late 1930s. Hard surfacing started with the steeper, eastern corridor, with seven miles of the road—including the section from the top of West Bluff on down to Copper Harbor—being paved in 1938. The final, unpaved, two miles of the road—located at the western terminus or "Silver River" end of the route—was hard surfaced two years later, in the summer of 1940.

Interestingly, the mountain drive has never actually been "paved," at least not in terms of asphalt being applied to its surface. Rather, the road has always had "road mix" applied to it. "Road mix" is a built-in-place mixture of gravel and tar that is blended, bladed out, and rolled in place, with the resulting surface then being seal coated. The "road mix" process is cost effective—it is something which the KCRC can do itself—in contrast to having to bring in an asphalt paving contractor. The process befits a "county road"—which is what Brockway Mountain Drive is—and is identical to the treatment applied to, for example, the Gay-Lac La Belle Road.

In terms of commercial development, Harold Wescoat recognized that the opening of the mountain drive would result in additional tourist dollars being brought to the area. After purchasing the top of West Bluff, Wescoat built what would be the first tourist shop to occupy the scenic overlook, the appropriately named, "Skytop Inn." The first "Skytop" was a rustic log cabin structure with a wrap-around observation deck; it lasted 30 years before finally yielding to the elements.

As Clyde Wescoat, Harold's grandson, reminisced relative to the long-running family business:

> "The first Skytop was built in 1935. In the fall of 1964, we dismantled it—we took out the windows, we 'bashed out' the big piece of float copper that was in the fireplace—it was completely cleaned out. We poured 5 gallons of fuel oil on the floor and lit it. It was a foggy, misty, late October day—it was an old creosoted structure and it really went up—in 3 hours, it was gone. The foundation for the new Skytop Inn went in and then, in spring, 1965, construction started on the upper part of the new building—the second Skytop Inn—the building that is there today. It was up and running that summer."

In a different sort of commercial venture, Harold Wescoat and Copper Harbor businessman, Joe Latoski, attempted to operate a ski hill off of the "eastern end," of the mountain during the winter of 1942–43. At the time, Mount Ripley Ski Hill was shut down because of World War II. Not much is known about this endeavor, however, it apparently never operated past its first winter.

The idea of a ski operation at the "eastern end" was tried again after World War II, this time by Copper Harbor businessman Percy Woods. As Percy's son, Bill Woods, recalled:

View from "Beaver Dam" Overlook, late 1930s.
Credit: Paul LaVanway Collection

View of West Bluff and southern ravine. Probably taken from "West Cracked Rock" or "Cracked Rock;" mid 1940s.
Credit: Paul LaVanway Collection

End of "Hartman's View", start of "Big Curve." This photo taken from same location as the photo located at the bottom of page 17, only three years later. Note: 1) Lack of vegetation (especially as compared to today); 2) "Washboarding" of gravel road; 3) Restart of single, stand-alone, rubble stone "rock guard rails" on right. About 1937–1938. *Credit: Paul LaVanway Collection*

Entrance to Brockway's View, 1940s. Notice that the path of an earlier Brockway road—possibly the remnants of a work road used during 1933 construction—is visible at the bottom left of the photo, just on the other side of the white and black road posts. *Credit: Clyde Wescoat Collection*

"At the time, Dad ran the DX Gas Station in Copper Harbor and had a small café and rented out a few rooms to tourists. But, in the winter, it was slim pickings. Dad just didn't have enough to do—that's how he got involved in the idea of getting the ski hill up and running again. Dad ran it during the winters of 1946–47 and 1947–48; at the time I was in high school and quite a few of my friends came out from Calumet to try it. Dad had set up a rope tow that ran up along the side of the road—it ran from the bottom of the hill on up to just short of the curve at Brockway's Nose—it was powered by an old Ford Model A motor; it had earlier been used in a sawmill, but Dad had modified it to run a tow rope. The people who went up, well, they would ski right down the middle of the road—the big trick was to make the corner at the bottom. Dad had picked up a bunch of skis that were war surplus and rented them out. The problem was there just were never enough people around to make a go of the operation. Just, not enough people."

Then there are the observations of long time Copper Harbor resident, Paul Bergh. Bergh worked as a Keweenaw County Sheriff's Deputy back in the days (i.e., 1939–1946) when his mother, Ida, had been Sheriff.

"Mom and I, well, we used to go up to the mountain drive and watch for speeders, but the thing was, there were never any speed limits posted—for that matter, to this day—there still aren't any speed limits posted. I guess we were just concerned about people driving safely. I suppose you could say that the nature and design of the road was such that the 'problem' of people driving too fast, driving dangerously, well, it was basically 'self-correcting.' And maybe, it was people taking their time—appreciating nature—that caused them to slow down. After all, the road—well, it is the crown jewel of the Keweenaw."

Certainly, the construction of a road across the spine of the Keweenaw stands as a unique event in the history of the Copper Country. It was a challenge met, as engineers and laborers faced and overcame significant obstacles.

Before the road, only a small number of people could enjoy the spectacular scenery—the natural beauty—that was "opened up" and made accessible because

View of Copper Harbor from "Brockway's View." About mid 1930s.
Credit: Paul LaVanway Collection

View of West Bluff from Keweenaw Mountain Lodge, early 1940s.
Credit: Paul LaVanway Collection

View of Lake Bailey, just below Lakeshore Drive, probably mid 1930s. Note that the caption accompanying this photograph depicts the scene as being "along the Mountain Drive;" this stems from the fact that Brockway Mountain Drive was opened to traffic (October 14, 1933), a full year before Lakeshore Drive was opened to vehicles. (October 12, 1934). *Credit: Paul LaVanway Collection*

Keweenaw County Road Commission signage at top of West Bluff. Mid 1940s.
Credit: Paul LaVanway Collection

SKYTOP INN

Erecting the floor structure of the first Skytop Inn. The Skytop was constructed by Ed Ackley and Silas Remillard, both of whom worked building the clubhouse at the Keweenaw Mountain Lodge. Fall, 1935. *Credit: Clyde Wescoat Collection*

Skytop Inn construction, view from north. Note that there are no "rock guard rails" present along the southern perimeter of the summit loop road in this photograph. Lake Medora visible in the background. Fall, 1935. *Credit: Clyde Wescoat Collection*

Skytop Inn construction: Harold Wescoat on left. Note that both KCRC signage and roadside roof of gazebo are visible in the background of this photograph. *Credit: Clyde Wescoat Collection*

Skytop Inn fireplace/chimney construction by stone mason Louis Azzi. Azzi also constructed the clubhouse fireplaces at the Keweenaw Mountain Lodge. Propbably spring, 1936. *Credit: Clyde Wescoat Collection*

View of Skytop Inn from roadside gazebo, located near the northeast corner of the summit loop road. This photograph appears to be a "double" exposure.
Credit: Clyde Wescoat Collection

Another view of nearly completed Skytop Inn. Note that "rock guard rails" are not present in background of this photograph. Probably Spring, 1936.
Credit: Clyde Wescoat Collection

Completed Skytop Inn. Note that single, stand-alone, rubble stone "rock guard rails" are visible along the perimeter of the summit of loop road in this photograph. Adrian Tousigant standing adjacent to doorway. Late 1930s.
Credit: Paul LaVanway Collection

Northeastern view of the Skytop Inn, top of West Bluff. Late 1930s.
Credit: Paul LaVanway Collection

the mountain drive was built. Indeed, the project has made for splendid experiences for the tens of thousands who come to the Keweenaw each year.

The building of the mountain drive represents a singular accomplishment by a generation which is rapidly succumbing to the effects of time. In point of fact, in performing the research for this article, it proved impossible to locate even a single individual who had worked on the original construction of the road. It was not much easier to find individuals who merely remembered the project taking place.

And so, as the mountain drive turns 75, the end of an era is at hand. Much as T. H. Watkins wrote in his narrative history of the depression, *The Hungry Years*: "A generation of witnesses is passing. The men and women who came to maturity during the years of one of the most transforming decades in American history are swiftly being lost to time, and the Great Depression, for so long a genuine memory in the lives of millions, will soon become fokelore—or fokelore's more respectable cousin, history."

This is to acknowledge Paul Bergh, Bob Carlton, Bill Clark, Steve D'Agostino, Steve DeFour, Jim Heikkila, Stan Martin, Clarence Monette, Gregg Patrick, Joe Waananen, Clyde Wescoat, Bill Woods, and Don Zappa for the assistance which they provided in the course of researching this subject.

Sky Top Inn

The poets write of enchanted days
and nights with a silvery moon,
of bark canoes on lakes and bays
where lovers softly croon.

But, give me Brockways lofty height
where lakes in its shadows lie:
The winding trail, a gorgeous sight,
so near to God on high.

Storms may come and storms may go,
and the heart may storm within:
but there's peace of soul, when you reach the goal,
The shelter of the Sky Top Inn.

Adrinne Tousignant

END NOTES

1. A few years following the completion of Brockway Mountain Drive, the Keweenaw County Road Commission (KCRC) revisited the idea of constructing a road to the top of Mount Lookout, (sometimes called Mount Baldy by Eagle Harbor residents), the same which is located immediately to the south of Lake Bailey. That said it is not clear whether the proposed project would have been linked to and/or could be considered to be a continuation of the Brockway Mountain Drive route. According to KCRC's Board of Road Commissioners meeting minutes for July 14, 1939: "Commissioner (Wesley H.) Clark reported that Calumet and Hecla had rejected the Commission's request for an easement for the construction of a road from Eagle Harbor to Mount Lookout." As an aside, but in a similar vein, Calumet and Hecla, around this same time, also rejected KCRC requests for easements which would have enabled construction of two other roads, one from Lake Medora to Bete Grise and another, from Gay to Lac La Belle.

2. Further to the question as to the proper name of "West Bluff," Keweenaw County Road Commission Board meeting minutes for June 12, 1936, indicate: "It was moved and supported that the name of West Bluff be changed to Mount Keweenaw and that the Clerk request the (Keweenaw County) Board of Supervisors to pass a resolution regarding same. Motion Passed. Yeas-Chairman Hartman, Members Potter and Clark. Nays-None. Carried."

3. Several months following completion of the first edition of the "Brockway Mountain Drive Story," Bill Clark recalled another intriguing incident concerning his father's work as an engineer on the Brockway Mountain Drive construction project. As Clark related, "One night Dad came home—and his pockets—the pockets of his pants and his coat—were just stuffed with agates. He couldn't have gotten any more in them if he tried—they were nice ones, too—just huge. I remember at the time him saying that they had been working on the stretch of road adjacent to Agate Harbor and in the course of clearing the roadway, they ran into a solid vein of agates. To this day I'm not sure exactly where the vein was, other than along Brockway, adjacent to Agate Harbor. It is probably buried under the road somewhere. For years I've wondered if that same vein of agates—which I'd bet probably extends out to the shore of Lake Superior—isn't the reason for the name 'Agate' in Agate Harbor."

4. Brockway Mountain Drive's first set of "rock guard rails," i.e., the walls made of cut and fitted fieldstone, were constructed in 1934. Originally, it was believed that the stone walls located along the U. S. 41 perimeter of the Keweenaw Mountain Lodge were built at the same time. Further research revealed that the rock walls at the Keweenaw Mountain Lodge were, in fact, constructed somewhat later. Both Works Progress Administration (WPA) records and contemporary newspaper accounts confirm that the stone walls at the Keweenaw Mountain Lodge were constructed in fall, 1940, and that this work was done coincident with the first hard surfacing of US 41. (See: *Daily Mining Gazette*: August 16, 1940, page 10; August 23, 1940, page 8; and, August 31, 1940, page 8.)

5. It was originally thought that the steeper, eastern corridor of the Mountain Drive—from the top of West Bluff on down to Copper Harbor—was hard surfaced in 1938, with the western side of the road not being paved until 1946, after the end of World War II. KCRC and WPA records helped to clarify the history of the matter. It now appears that the eastern seven miles of the route was paved in 1938, while the remainder of the road—the western end of the road, including the path of the earlier Military Road—was hard surfaced in 1940. WPA project records indicate that a total of 23,720 cubic yards of "oil aggregate surface road mix" were applied to the surface of Brockway Mountain Drive in the course of the 1938 hard surfacing project. Keweenaw County Road Commission minutes of June 14, 1940, indicate: "The Board has been notified that the WPA will furnish 30,000 gallons of road oil during the month of June. This oil will be used to complete the surfacing of the Mountain Drive and the remainder will be used on the Village Streets."

6. WPA records indicated that the second type of "rock guard rails"—the set of 66 individual, stand alone, rubble stone walls—the walls that are topped with a formed and poured concrete cap—were constructed in 1937. Interestingly, one of the individuals who worked building these "second generation" walls—a Waino Niemela—contacted the author and was able to provide a number of interesting insights on the stand alone "rock guard rail" construction process.

According to Niemela, "…prebuilt rough lumber forms were used to build the walls. We'd dig down through the top soil—what little of it that there was—all the way down to bedrock—and then we'd set up the form. We'd pour cement on the ground as a base and then start piling rocks into the form—adding more cement in the middle—then more rocks—until we got to the top of the form. The next day, after all the cement dried, we'd pull off the form and move on to the next section. There was another crew who came along after us—they were always 'chasing us'—and poured the concrete cap."

Niemela elaborated: "You'll notice that they (i.e., the later stone walls) typically appear in groups of threes—that's because we had three forms. A lot of times, too, the walls ended up tilted or a bit 'cock-eyed'—that was because the wooden forms were bolted together and didn't have a lot of 'give' to them. The later walls—the ones we built—didn't turn out looking anywhere near as good as the first walls that were built. On the other hand, the WPA was able to get away on the cheap—they just paid us as laborers—not like having to pay a stone mason. A stone mason, now they were 'king of the hill' when it came to wages." [Records indicate that hourly wages paid on KCRC-sponsored WPA projects in 1937 were: Laborers-.365; Trades Helpers-.48; Carpenters, Plumbers & Electricians-.715; Stone Mason-$1.50]

Keweenaw County Road Commission-WPA Project Proposal records indicate that KCRC unsuccessfully requested approval from WPA on several different occasions to increase the number of "rubble guard rail" walls on Brockway Mountain Drive. [e.g. the addition of 3,000 linear feet of rubble guard rail was requested as Sponsor's Proposal No. 8, dated June 28, 1939-State of Michigan Local Project No. 42-5-2028]. [Also, as an aside, requests by KCRC to WPA to finance widening of the roadway, from 18' to 28', were, similarly, never approved]. The failure of the Road Commission to obtain funding from WPA to construct additional stone walls likely led directly to the erection of the cable guard rails that now span the upper reaches of the western side of the Brockway route—the wire rope guard rails that are in place today; KCRC records document the construction of these safety barriers in 1939.

7. At the summit of West Bluff, there is evidence of concrete bases that were used to provide support for both a flag pole (i.e., extreme southwest corner of summit loop road) and coin-operated telescopic binocular stations (i.e., north side of summit loop road). The flag pole foundation probably dates to the 1937–1939 era and was likely the result of work performed under the auspices of the WPA. The coin operated telescopic binocular bases date to the mid-1950s; KCRC Board meeting minutes of March 12, 1954, indicate that the Board, "…approved placing telescopic type 'viewing machines' along the right-of-ways at Owl's Creek (i.e., Great Sand Bay), Brockway Mountain Drive and Grand Marais overlooks, with the understanding that the vendor, Mr. Donald J. Curley of Lake Linden, would pay the Commission 5% of the gross receipts."

8. The first to operate the Skytop Inn was Adrian Tousigant; Tousigant is the lady pictured standing adjacent the doorway of the Skytop in the late-1930s photo on page 19. Other individuals who have worked at the Skytop include Jimmy Abrams, Jim Wescoat, Mac Frimodig, Marilyn MacKerroll Wescoat, Florence Wescoat Jens, Susie Jens Evanoff, Barbara Simila, Marsha Heur and Clyde H. Wescoat. If there were an award for longest service at the Skytop, it would unquestionably belong to Lloyd Tucker Wescoat, who has operated the shop more or less continuously since 1981.

Maps, Diagrams, and Route Finder

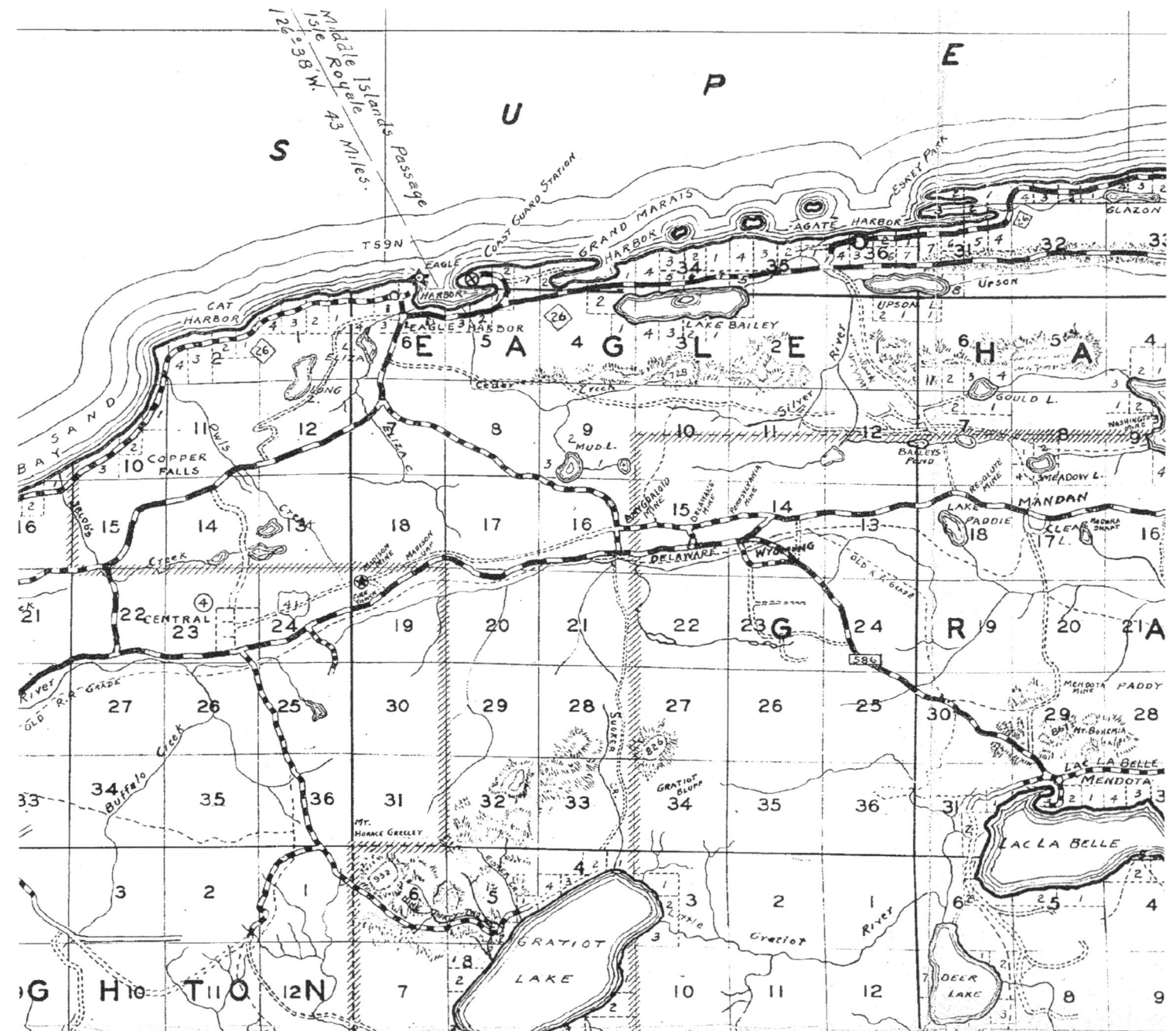

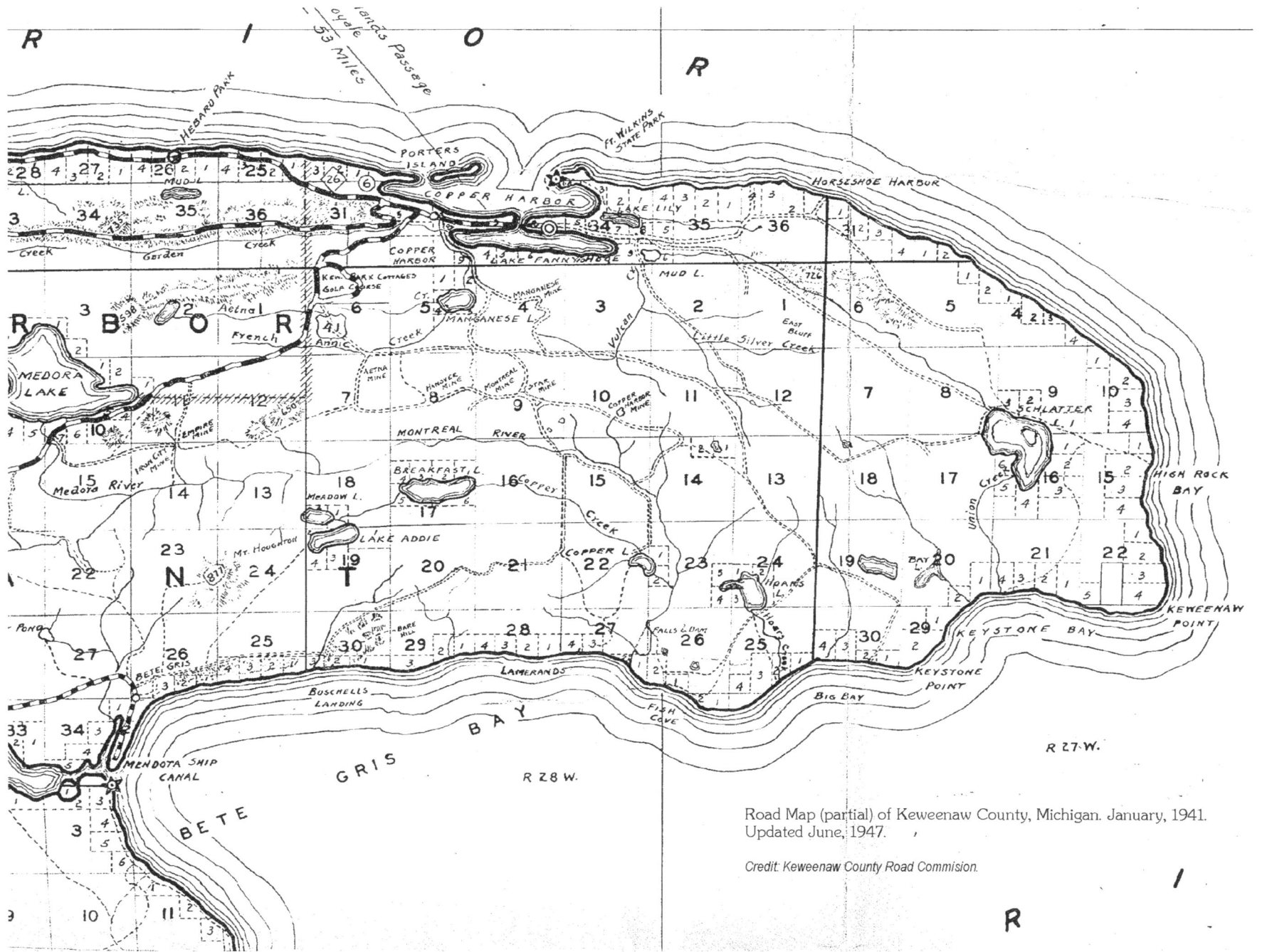

Road Map (partial) of Keweenaw County, Michigan. January, 1941. Updated June, 1947.

Credit: Keweenaw County Road Commision.

LAKE SUPERIOR

T 59 N

Row (top, sections 34–35 along shore):
- 34 Grand Marais — Goodell / Cal. + Hecla
- 35 Boston + L.S. Copp. Co. / Mrs. A. Scott
- 36 Eagle Park — Mrs. A. Scott
- 31 Schmidt / Boston Mineral Land Co.
- 32 Boston and Lake Sup. / Boston Mineral Land Co.
- 33 Pethrick / Boston (and Lake Sup.)
- 34 Vaughn / Dakin
- 35 Hebbard / Cole, Nichols, Badger
- (far right) Hebbard, Longyear

Agate Harbor, Upson Lake, Chas. Hebbard

6 Cal. + Hecla	5 Cal. + Hecla	4 Cal. + Hecla	3 Boston + Lake Super. Mineral Land Co. / Native Copper Co.	2 Keweenaw Assoc. Ltd. / Keweenaw Copper Co.	1 Keweenaw Copper Co.	6 H.S. Badger / Keweenaw Copper Co.	5 Keweenaw Copper Co. / Washington Mng. Co.	4 St. Marys Canal Co. / Washington Mng. Co.	3 St. Marys Canal Co. / Keweenaw Copper	2 St. Marys Canal Co. / Keweenaw Copper	1 Keweenaw Copper Co.

Eagle Harbor, Lake Bailey

| 7 Cal. + Hecla | 8 Cal. + Hecla | 9 Cal. + Hecla | 10 F.W. Nichols / Native Copper Co. | 11 C+H / Keweenaw Copper / New Jersey Mng. Co. | 12 Keweenaw Copper / Cal. + Hecla | 7 Keweenaw Copper | 8 Keweenaw Copp / Washington Mng. Co. | 9 Washington Mng. Co. | 10 Mosquito Lake / Keweenaw Copper Co. | 11 Wash. Mng. / Keweenaw Copper Co. | 12 Hussey Howe |

| 18 Cal. + Hecla | 17 Cal. + Hecla | 16 Cal. + Hecla (Delaware) | 15 Cal. + Hecla | 14 Cal. + Hecla / New Jersey Mng. Co. | 13 New Jersey Mng. Co. / Cal. + Hecla | 18 Keweenaw Copp. Co. | 17 Keweenaw Copp. Co. | 16 Emma Mason | 15 Keweenaw Copp. Co. / Boston + Lake Super. Mng. Co. | 14 Keweenaw Copp. Co. | 13 St. Marys Can. |

| 19 Cal. + Hecla | 20 Cal. + Hecla | 21 Cal. + Hecla | 22 Chapman / Cal. + Hecla | 23 Cal. + Hecla / H. Johnson | 24 Cal. + Hecla | 19 St. Marys Canal Co. / Keweenaw Copp Co. | 20 Cal. + Hecla / Keweenaw Copp. Co. | 21 Cal. + Hecla / Boston + Lake Superior Mng. Co. | 22 Cal. + Hecla | 23 St. Marys Canal Co. | 24 St. Marys Can. |

| 30 Cal. + Hecla | 29 Cal. + Hecla | 28 Cal. + Hecla | 27 Cal. + Hecla / Nichols, Cole + Foley | 26 Cal. + Hecla / Nichols, Cole + Foley | 25 Cal. + Hecla | 30 Cal. + Hecla | 29 Cal. + Hecla | 28 Cal. + Hecla / St. Marys Canal Co. | 27 St. Marys Canal Co. | 26 St. Marys Canal Co. / W.H. Fawcett | 25 St. Marys Can. |

| 31 | 32 Cal. + Hecla / St. Marys Canal Co. | 33 C+H / Nichols Cole + Foley / St. Marys Canal Co. | 34 Cal. + Hecla / Nichols, Cole + Foley / Nichols + Taylor / St. Marys Canal Co. | 35 Nichols, Cole + Foley / St. Marys Canal Co. | 36 Cal. + Hecla | 31 Cal. + Hecla | 32 Cal. + Hecla | 33 Cal. + Hecla | 34 Cal. + Hecla | C+H / W. Fawcett / T. Hodgson | BETE |

LAC LA BELLE

R 30 W   R 29 W

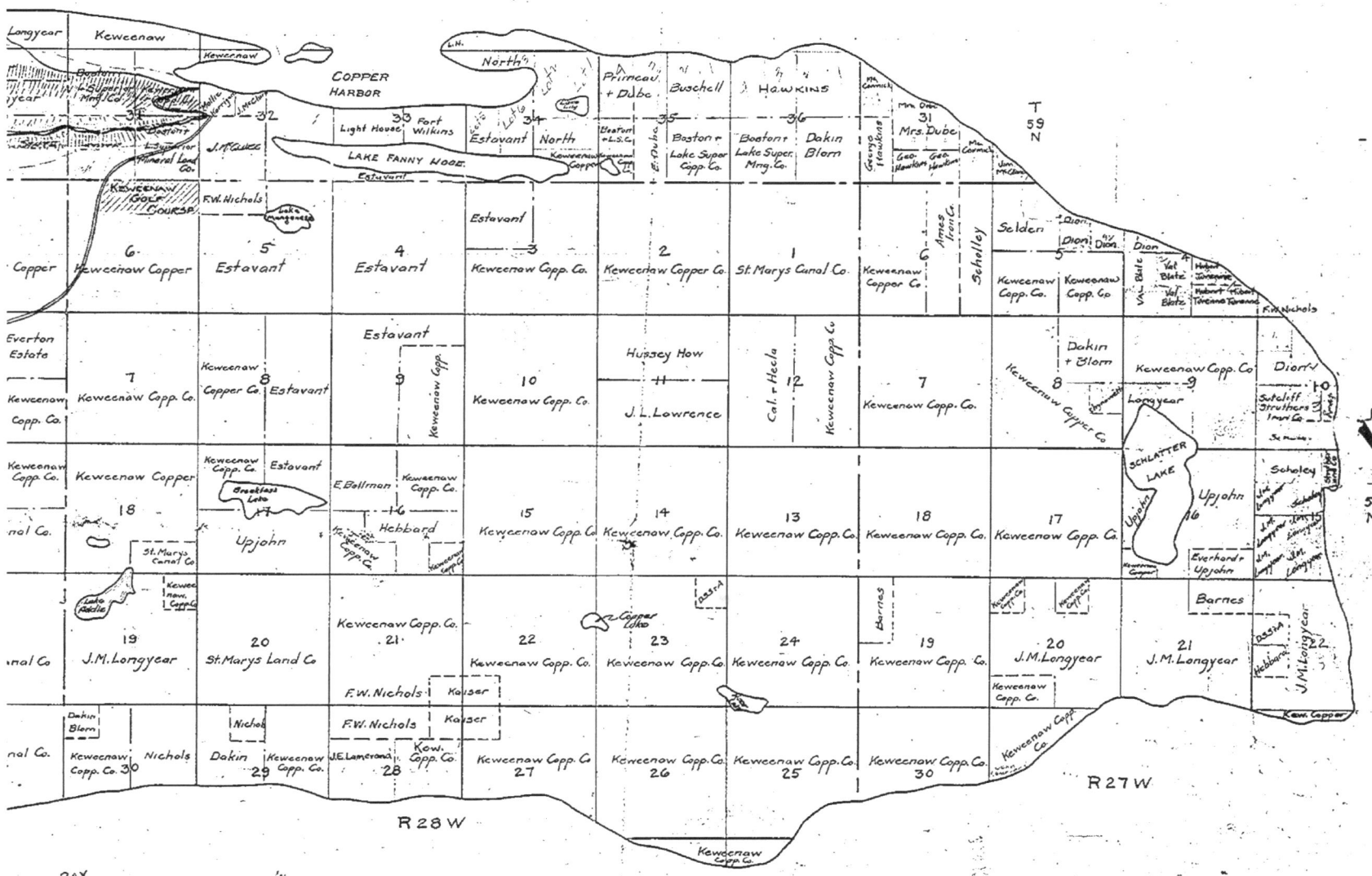

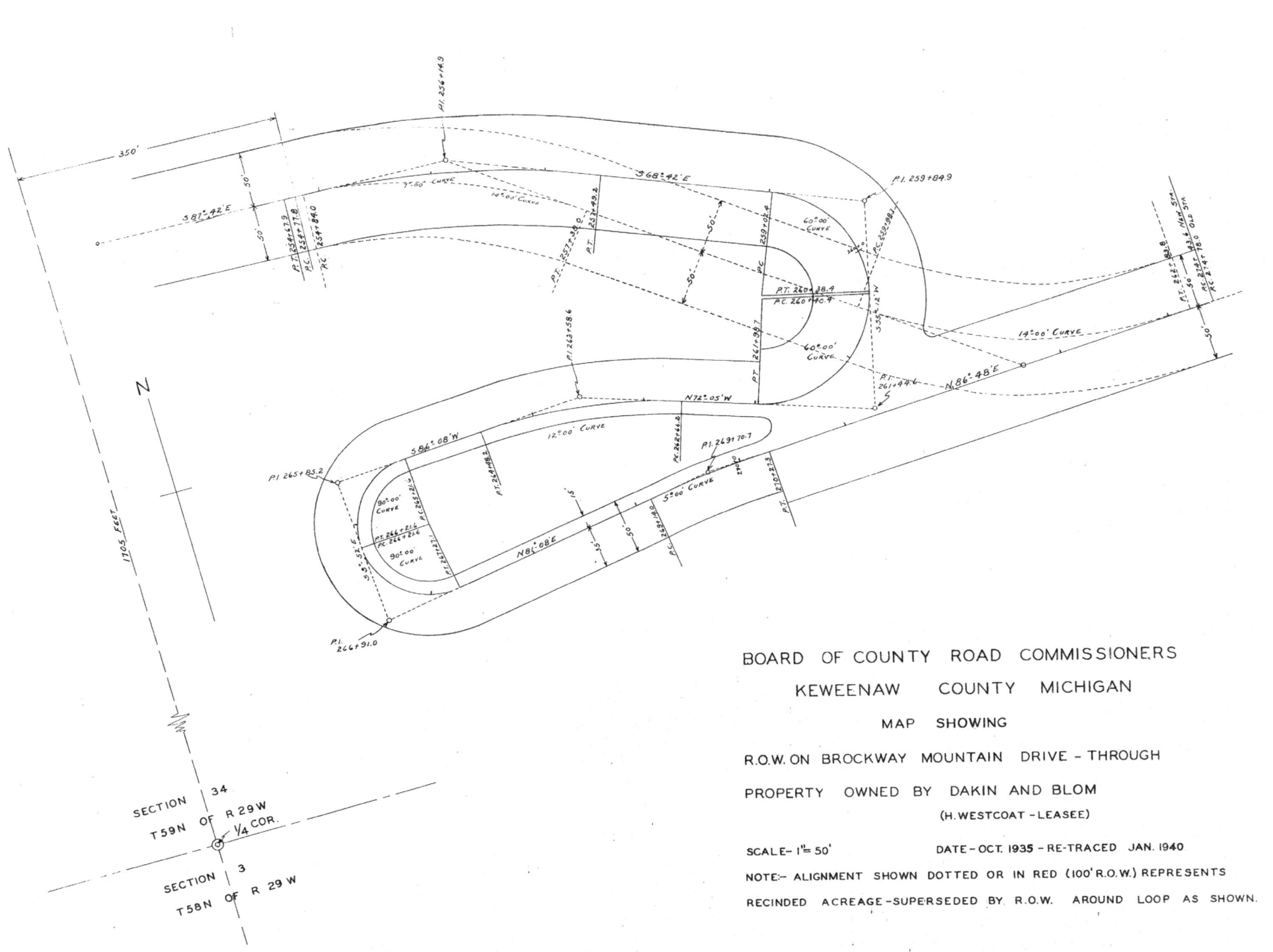

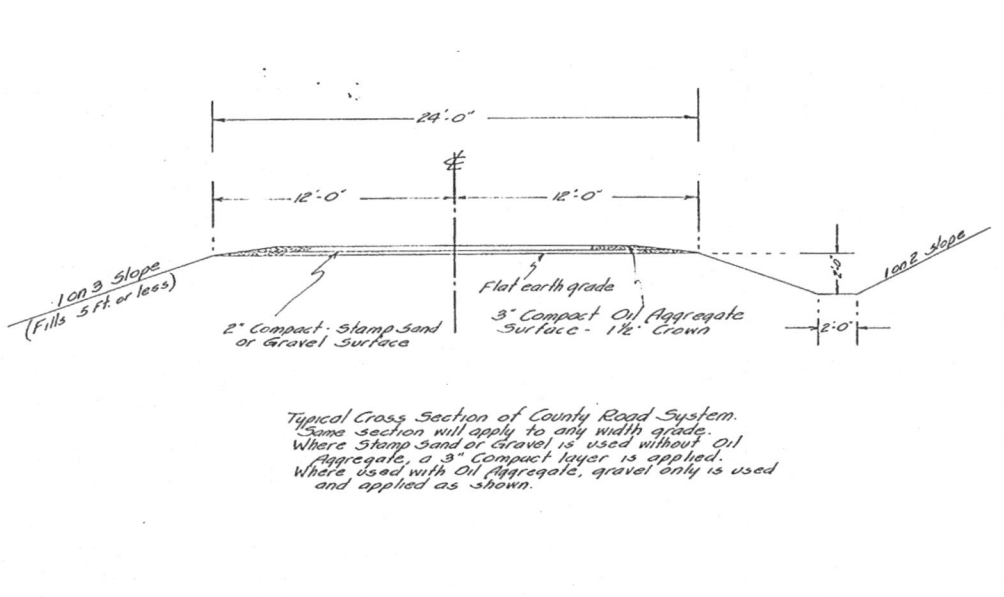
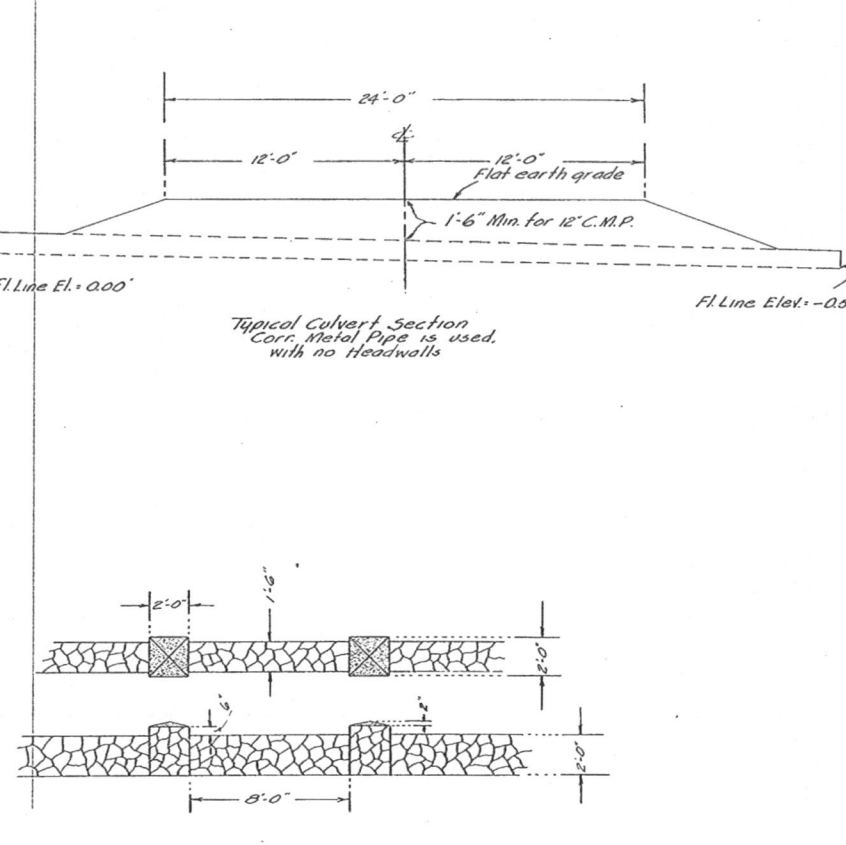
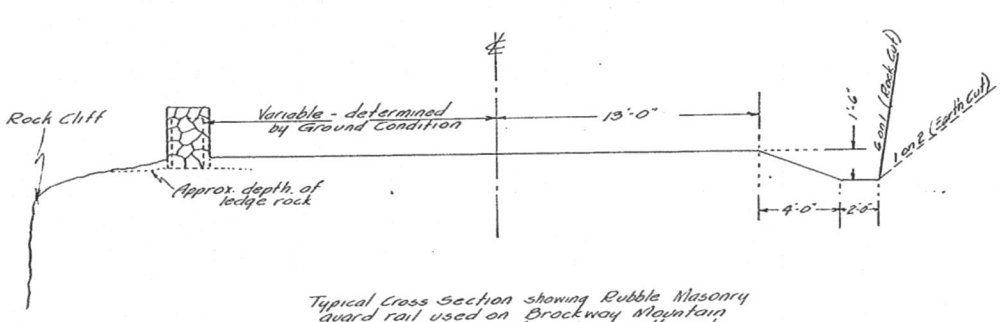
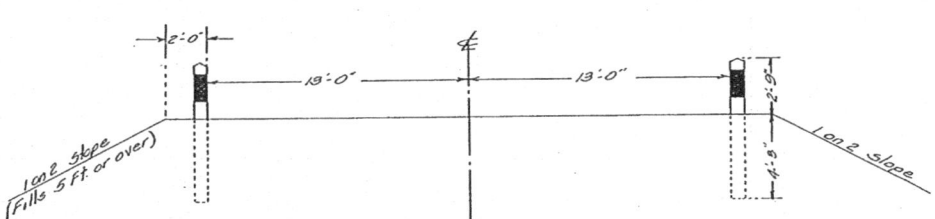

**BOARD OF COUNTY ROAD COMMISSIONERS
KEWEENAW COUNTY – MICHIGAN**
Standard Cross Sections
Used On All County Roads
Scale – ¼" = 1'

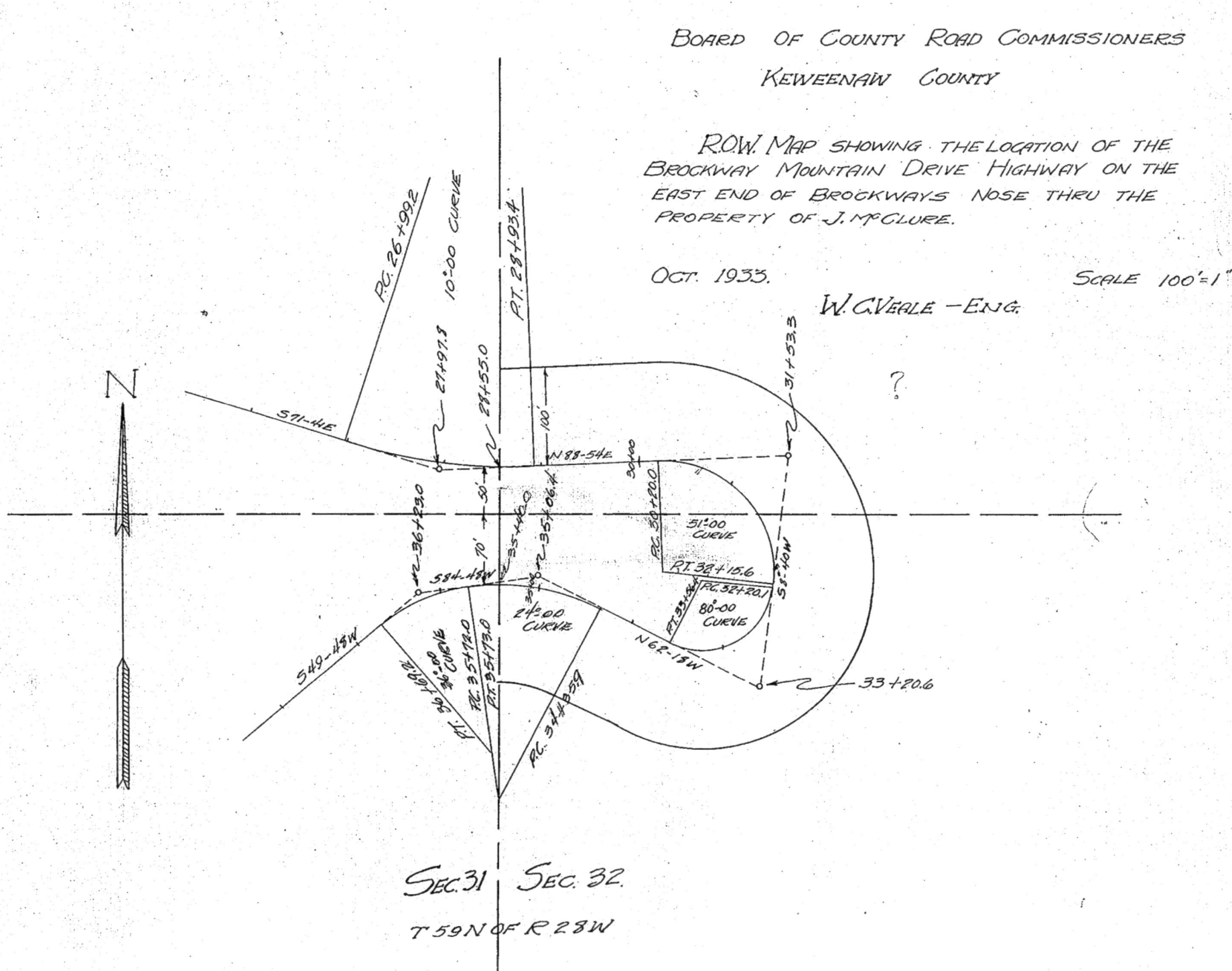

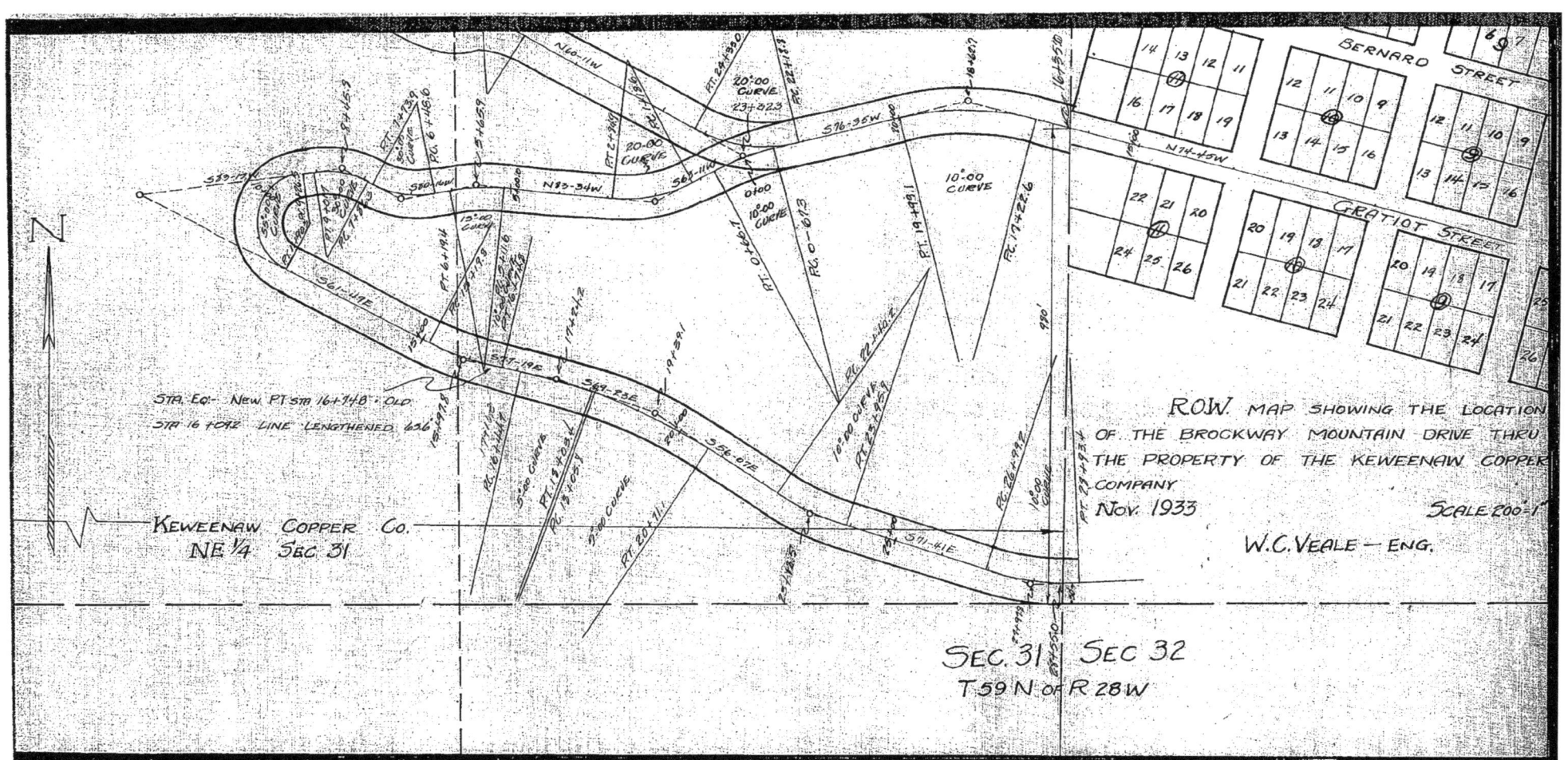

Route Finder-Brockway Mountain Drive (BMD)
Note: Mileages Are Approximate

>Begin at the Silver River (i.e., Eagle Harbor or western) end of Brockway Mountain Drive at M-26

>0.2 miles	Remnants of the former Resolute Road are clearly evident on both the north and south sides of BMD. At this point, BMD follows what was originally the route of the "Fort Wilkins (Copper Harbor, MI) to Fort Howard (Green Bay, WI) Military Road."	The Resolute Mining Company was organized in 1864 and worked a fissure vein until 1867. The company built a wagon road from their pier on Lake Superior along the path of what is now the Silver River Loop Road. The road then ran along the path of the adjacent power line, running up, over and across BMD. Resolute Road then continued out to the company mine site, which was located adjacent to what is today US 41, between Delaware and Mandan.
>0.6 miles	Michigan Nature Association (MNA) Upson Lake Sanctuary signage on right.	
>2.2 miles	On right, flood-related forest damage caused by beaver damming flow of Upson Creek.	
>2.6 miles	Original path of the Military Road, constructed 1864-71, veers off to the right, today, a "two track."	Up to this point, Brockway is a forest drive; it begins to alter character, starting a very gradual, steady, rise in elevation. Upson Creek valley starts to appear on the right side of the road. First of 3 strand cable guardrail, constructed from copper mining-era wire rope, (dates to 1939 construction on the road), appears on right.
>2.7 miles	Michigan Audubon Society Brockway Mountain Sanctuary signage on left.	
>3.1 miles	Trail to Bill Mattila's mountain-top "shack" to left.	Mattila, who died in 1985, was the "hermit" of Brockway Mountain, living a more or less solo existence on the ridge-top for 32 years.
>4.7 miles	Old trail to borrow pit located on right side of road.	This trail is over-grown with vegetation and is easily missed. The trail leads to a borrow pit, now private property, that is located at the base of West Bluff. The pit was a source for obtaining a clay-type of fill material used in construction of the original roadbed.

>5.0 miles	Turn off to West Bluff and scenic road loop providing access to overlook at top of Brockway Mountain Drive. Overlook is 726 above the mean level of Lake Superior and 1328 feet above sea level. On a clear day, to the northwest, both Isle Royale and the curvature of the Earth are readily apparent. Agate Harbor and Eagle Harbor (Note, in far distance, the "speck" of the alternating red and white flashing light from beacon of Eagle Harbor Lighthouse) visible along shoreline to WNW. Keweenaw ridgeline visible to west, while Lake Medora and Mount Bohemia visible to south.	Remnants from earlier commercial development at West Bluff remain along the loop road, including a concrete flag pole base (at extreme SW corner), concrete base for a coin operated binocular (near NW corner), and fieldstone fireplace base for the first "Skytop Inn" (center). The southern escarpment of West Bluff is "surrounded" by 27, stand-alone, individual rubble stone "rock guard rails," each 10' in length. These walls are topped with a "formed and poured concrete cap" and are mostly constructed of a dark gray, basalt-type, rock—similar to what might be found at Central Mine. (Note: Several of the rocks in these walls contain drill holes). These walls were probably constructed ca. 1937 as a WPA project.
>5.1 miles	"Steep Hill Down" road sign on right leads to what original road builders called "East Valley."	
>5.5 miles	Early road plans referenced this spot as the "first topographic hill east of west bluff." However, it soon assumed the moniker "East Hill."	Located directly across from MNA's James Klipfel Memorial Sanctuary and Trail, this marks the start of the "piered" walls—stone walls constructed from cut and fitted fieldstone—and which are topped with a "concrete wash." These are the earliest walls constructed on Brockway and were erected ca. 1934 by Keweenaw County Road Commission (KCRC) employees. (Note: These walls, in terms of style, are very similar to those that had been constructed a few years earlier at Glacier National Park in NW Montana—and would be constructed in 1940 along the US 41 perimeter of Keweenaw Mountain Lodge.)
>6.0 miles	Originally, "Beaver Dam Overlook." (i.e., the wall area with "angled" end sections)	Originally a wall with 7 "piers", this wall was damaged by vandals, hence, the "stand-alone" pier at the east end of this overlook.
>6.3 miles	Originally called "West Cracked Rock" and "Cracked Rock" Overlooks (i.e., the "curved" or "rounded" wall with 11 piers)	A stone wall section of 32 piers with adjacent "piered" wall sections, (to the west), of 7 piers and, (to the east), of 11 piers, this is the second longest section of early or "piered" stone walls on Brockway. On a moderately clear day, the north and south "sides" of Lake Superior, as it surrounds the Keweenaw Peninsula, is readily visible in the eastern horizon.
>6.8 miles	Bottom of "Birch Valley."	The bottom of Birch Valley is marked by 7 white posts along the right hand side of the road.
>7.1 miles	Unidentified Overlook	Stone wall overlook having 32 "piers." Mt. Houghton visible in the southern horizon.

>7.3 miles	Early road descriptions and plans identify this low spot as, "Kettle Gulch."	
>7.5 miles	Originally called "Hartman's View" overlook.	Named for Wm. F. Hartman, who was Chairman of the KCRC in the early 1930s. With 69 piers and covering 818 feet, this is the single longest section of the early or "piered" stone wall on Brockway. Both Keweenaw Mountain Lodge and the curves of US 41 are readily apparent to the south. A stamp sand storage field was located across the road from the western end of Hartman's View and served as a materials staging area during the 1978 resurfacing of the east side of BMD.
>7.6 miles		Individual, stand-alone, rubble stone "rock guard rails," each with a "formed and poured concrete cap" start again. There are 39 "individual" walls in this section, each 10' long; they are constructed using a combination of rubble stone and poor rock. Probably constructed ca. 1937, at the same time that the single, stand-alone, walls at the summit of West Bluff were built.
>8.1 miles	Called the "Big Curve" in early documents on Brockway.	Descent from "Hartman's View." In early photographs of Brockway, and prior to the growth of vegetation, Horseshoe Harbor, Copper Harbor and Lake Fanny Hooe are all prominently visible across the horizon, immediately to the east of this stretch of road. In the course of descending Big Curve, you will notice that on the extreme left hand side (or north side) of the road, immediately adjacent to the last few guard rail posts, the remnants of an earlier roadbed—possibly a Brockway Mountain Drive construction road—will be apparent.
>8.3 miles	"Scenic Lookout at Brockway's View;" sometimes called "Brockway's Nose"	This rounded curve replaced an earlier, "hairpin" curve—possibly a Brockway construction road; see commentary, above.
>8.7 miles	Bottom of Hill	Note significant drilling and blasting of rock face along this section of road, especially from "Brockway's View" on down to "Bottom of Hill," creating this, the steepest section of the BMD roadway.

>8.9 miles	Brockway Mountain Drive ends; road rejoins Lake Shore Drive, M-26 at Copper Harbor.	
		Total length of individual, stand alone type of rubble stone "rock guard rails" with "formed and poured concrete cap"=660'
		Total length of "piered" walls made of cut and fitted fieldstone, covered on top with a "concrete wash"=1,918'
		Total length of all types of stone walls=2,578'

Keweenaw Mountain Lodge Story

The Keweenaw Mountain Lodge is a recognized symbol of Upper Peninsula hospitality. Situated amidst the remote northern reaches of Michigan's Copper Country and framed by the mountainous splendor of the Keweenaw Peninsula, "the Lodge"—as it has come to be known to locals and visitors alike—is among the Keweenaw's most interesting and historically notable places.

Designed and constructed as a wilderness golf resort—in the midst of some of the Upper Midwest's most beautiful scenery—the legacy of the Lodge is one of friendly service, good food and affordable fun. Balancing history, hospitality and rustic elegance, the tranquility of the Lodge has long made it a favorite of those who prefer a relaxed environment and the charm of a bygone era.

View towards east of recently enclosed Clubhouse porch and main entrance, 1939–40. The location of this photograph was later the site of the bar and is now the location of the management and administrative offices. Note copper chandeliers, the same crafted in Calumet & Hecla's metal shop. Southern view

THE BACKDROP OF THE GREAT DEPRESSION

The Lodge owes its existence to the Great Depression. It was a time when Keweenaw County faced the greatest crisis in its history. The Great Depression, with all its terrible implications, had spread across America. And nowhere did it hit harder than in the Keweenaw.

Starting with the stock market crash of October, 1929, the county's copper mining industry—an industry which emerged prior to the Civil War, rose to dominance in the later years of the 19th century and started into decline following the First World War—began to fall silent.

Spring, 1930, found the Mohawk Mining Company closing down production, as soon as the first effects of the economic slowdown appeared. Then, on September 12, 1932, the company announced that it was permanently suspending all mining activities. Shortly thereafter, Mohawk commenced the process of liquidation. Affairs were equally bleak at the neighboring Ahmeek Mining Company. Spring, 1932 found Ahmeek—owned by the Calumet & Hecla Consolidated Copper Company (C&H)—laying off 700 men as it completely shut down mining operations; the enterprise would not resume activities until 1936.

All this occurred in a county which—according to the 1930 U.S. Census—had a total population of 5,076 people—about 1,000 families. While there are no consistent data for unemployment in Keweenaw County in the early 1930s, it is possible to gauge the extent of unemployment by examining relief aid data. In this regard, the State Emergency Welfare Relief Commission, Lansing, reported in July of 1933 that 75.2% of Keweenaw County's population was on relief—a greater percentage than any other county in Michigan. The situation in the Keweenaw was sufficiently dire that it even caught the attention of federal officials. Indeed, it was Harry Hopkins—one of President Franklin Roosevelt's closest, most trusted advisors and architect of the New Deal's relief programs—who reported that Michigan's Copper Country had the highest relief load in the nation.

Prior to the New Deal and its transformation of the American social welfare system, public relief was almost exclusively a function of local government. In Keweenaw County, providing relief to the local population and work to the

US 41 adjacent to Lake Medora—May 2, 1928. The Keweenaw County Road Commission rebuilt US 41 between Delaware and Copper Harbor during the Winter of 1931–32, utilizing 275 men assigned by the KCRC Road Relief Department."

unemployed was the responsibility of the Keweenaw County Road Commission (KCRC). In fact, in the early 1930s, so closely intertwined were the concepts of "relief" and "road work," that the County welfare office operated under the name "Road Relief Department."

Among the first Depression-era road projects in which the Keweenaw County Road Commission became involved—using labor assigned by the KCRC-administered Road Relief Department—was the 1931–32 rebuild and upgrading of US 41 between Delaware and Copper Harbor. A remnant of this project is the rock wall façade which parallels the eastern side of US 41 between the Lodge and Copper Harbor. At the time, unemployed miners blasted away the hillside to lower the grade and improve the safety of this otherwise dangerous section of highway.

The summer of 1932 found the U. S. presidential election campaign taking place in an atmosphere in which the effects of the Great Depression were felt intensely across the nation. President Herbert Hoover's popular support began to deteriorate as voters felt that he was unable to reverse the economic decline. Franklin Delano Roosevelt, promising "a new deal for the American people," ended up winning the contest by a landslide margin.

Sworn in on March 4, 1933—in the midst of the worst bank panic in U.S. history—FDR's inauguration signified the inception of a significant shift—possibly even a generational realignment—in political and domestic policy. With Roosevelt's inauguration came increased federal control over the economy—the beginning of economic activism—and the building of a comparatively larger and more complex social welfare system.

Among the first direct-relief programs begun under the New Deal was FERA—the Federal Emergency Relief Administration. Established on May 12, 1933, with passage of the Federal Emergency Relief Act, FERA gave states and localities money to alleviate the effects of adult unemployment by operating local relief programs. However, while FERA provided federal relief funding to the states, it was generally less successful in providing people jobs.

Back in Keweenaw County, the Road Commission—overseen by a three member board comprised of Chairman William F. Hartman and members William F. "Bill" Bolley and Ocha Potter—led local efforts to provide work opportunities to the unemployed. Most notably, spring, 1933, found KCRC employing hundreds of men as it began construction of Brockway Mountain Drive. Soon thereafter, work commenced building Lakeshore Drive. It was at about this same time that KCRC Board Member Potter—nominally Superintendent of the then shuttered Ahmeek Mining Company—began serving as volunteer head of the Road Relief Department.

Ocha Potter, 1878–1955. Potter originated the idea and laid the groundwork for the Keweenaw Park and Golf Course project.

Wesley H. "Cy" Clark, 1888–1959. Clark was instrumental in the development of the "Cottages" project, enabling it to obtain WPA funding.

As spring, 1933, turned to summer and then autumn, continued high levels of national unemployment and concerns for public welfare during the upcoming winter resulted in President Roosevelt unveiling the Civil Works

Administration (CWA) program. Created under FERA, CWA projects, while federally funded, were primarily sponsored by local governments. Designed to create millions of construction and maintenance jobs, CWA was among the first public employment policy experiments of the New Deal. CWA was the adult employment equivalent of the Civilian Conservation Corps (CCC), taking recipients off of the "dole" and providing the unemployed—some of whom had not worked at a real job for years—work and regular wages.

Autumn 1933 found Ocha Potter intimately involved in helping to develop plans which would provide work opportunities to Keweenaw County's unemployed. It was not long before he received a telegram from the State Emergency Relief Office asking for the submission of ideas for public projects suitable for funding under the CWA program. In response, Potter proposed a project which would employ hundreds—the construction of a publicly-owned golf course and clubhouse—what became known as the Keweenaw Park and Golf Course.

Effectively, CWA had a relatively brief lifetime—only five months—terminating at the end of March, 1934. Yet, CWA proved to be an enormously popular program, creating public construction jobs and moving beyond traditional "make work" activities to projects of permanent value. In the process, it paved the way for another program—one which would succeed it just a few years later—the Works Progress Administration—the WPA.

The Keweenaw Park and Golf Course project, conceived as a Civil Works Administration program, was continued under the auspices of FERA; later, it was completed as a Works Progress Administration project. The resulting facility—some 30 years later—then operated by a private owner, would change its name, assuming the moniker by which it is known today—the Keweenaw Mountain Lodge.

THE PROJECT BEGINS

The project began with site selection. Late October, 1933, found the Road Commission Board—who on November 17, 1933, established themselves as the Board of Park Trustees of Keweenaw County—meeting with Walter B. Congdon and Charles A. Wright. Congdon and Wright were, respectively, President and Secretary of the Keweenaw Copper Company.

Keweenaw Park entrance road, spring, 1934. This view is looking down the road, towards US 41. Photograph was probably taken near to the curve where the tennis court was later constructed.

Preparing to pull stumps, number 2 fairway, spring, 1934. Roadway of US 41 would be to left in this photograph. Ridgeline of West Bluff and Brockway Mountain Drive is visible along horizon.

Southeast view of Clubhouse, December, 1934. Note the broadly pitched roof which continued around the front, back and sides of the Clubhouse, covering the open, gallery-like, porch.

The group reviewed several potential locations for the Keweenaw Park and Golf Course project. After considering several possibilities, a 167.27 acre parcel of land—about a quarter of a square mile—was selected. The chosen parcel, originally part of the Aetna Mining Company's lands, was owned by Aetna's successor, the Keweenaw Copper Company. The parcel was located about one mile southwest of Copper Harbor and was situated on a conglomerate plateau overlooking Lake Superior. The hilltop vantage point offered spectacular views of the surrounding ridges and valleys and was covered with thick stands of white pine, spruce, maple, and oak.

Keweenaw Park and Golf Course Opening Day Ceremony, June 23, 1935.

The spot was known to local residents as Sahl's Hill; it had been the home of Keweenaw pioneer settler and long-time resident, Joseph Sahl. Sahl had come to the Copper Country in the mid-1840s, soon after the territory had been opened to white settlement. Sahl had worked as a copper miner and, afterwards, during the 1870 to 1890 era, operated a small brewery. According to legend, Sahl was the principal supplier of "beverages" to French Annie's, a popular saloon and bordello. French Annie's was located just down the road—down what is today's US 41, what at the time was called the Mineral Range State Road—right where it crossed French Annie's Creek.

The understanding reached between the Keweenaw Copper Company and the Park Trustees provided for the donation of the 167 acre parcel to the County. The accord, however, was subject to several conditions. Among the stipulations was the requirement that a nine hole golf course be constructed by July 1, 1934, with a second nine holes—making for a complete 18 hole course—being built by July 1, 1935. The agreement sanctioned the removal of water from Aetna and/or French Annie Creeks, as might be necessary for operation of the golf course and support facilities; it also allowed for the use of immediately adjacent Keweenaw Copper Company lands for purposes of the building of a dam and/or water reservoir. Keweenaw Copper Company retained mineral rights to the property and conditioned the donation upon the on-going use of the parcel as a public park and golf course.

The written agreement between Keweenaw Copper and the Park Trustees—dated January 2, 1934—was extended and amended several times. Each extension and amendment was prompted by the Park Trustee's failure to fulfill the contractual requirement providing for the construction of the second nine holes of the golf course. Eventually—some five years after the initial agreement was inked—it became apparent that the construction of the second nine holes was improbable. A new agreement between Keweenaw Copper and the Board of Park Trustees was then concluded. Dated July 19, 1938, this accord provided for the outright sale of the surface rights to the 167 acre property for the sum of $1,500. Like the earlier accord, this deed contained the covenant that the premises "…be solely and exclusively used for the purpose of constructing, maintaining and operating a public park, including a golf course…forever."

View of Number 1 tee and fairway, mid 1930s.

In addition to the 167 acre Keweenaw Copper Company parcel, arrangements were made to lease several adjoining tracts, lands generally located to the north and to the west of the golf course. These same lands—comprising a 157.95 acre parcel located to the north of the golf course and a 160 acre "quarter section" situated to the northwest—would eventually be purchased by the Board of Park Trustees.

The Keweenaw Park and Golf Course site thus came to comprise an area of three-fourths of a square mile. It was this physical location, possibly more than any other factor, that would come to define the character of "the Lodge."

Photograph of Number 1 green, mid 1930s

View of Number 6 green, mid 1930s. Water hazard and water pump house are visible in background.

View of Number 2 fairway, mid 1930s. Note vehicle travelling on US 41; the stone wall bordering the edge of the Keweenaw Park and Golf Course property was not constructed until fall, 1940.

Site Work:

Work on the Keweenaw Park and Golf Course project began on Monday, November 6, 1933. Initially, a crew of 124 workmen—primarily of Finnish, Italian and English ancestry—was assigned to the project. The first work involved construction of a gravel entrance road and clearing of timber from the golf course fairways.

The site was surveyed by a team composed of Thomas Knight, John W. Jackson, Harry A. Swanson, and Wesley H. "Cy" Clark. Jackson, Swanson, and Clark all were surveyors and/or assistant engineers at KCRC. Knight was the youngest member of the survey party; it was his first job following his 1933 graduation as a mechanical engineer from Michigan College of Mining and Technology.

As work began and then progressed into the winter of 1933–34, the quiet of the northern forest was broken by the sound of axes and cross-cut saws busy at work. An estimated 18,700 trees were cut and 16,500 stumps blasted in the process of clearing the 18 fairways. Hundreds of softwood logs, primarily pine and spruce, were debarked, stacked, and saved for later construction of the Clubhouse. Three thousand cords of hardwood firewood, then valued at $4 a cord, were created from the timber clearing project; almost all of this was distributed to families on relief for use as fuel. Additionally, a building site for the proposed clubhouse was selected, cleared and leveled.

Copper Harbor summer resident Stan Martin recalled the 1934 site clearing work: "At the time, Dad was building our cabin in Copper Harbor and hired several of the same workmen who were employed up on the golf course project. The work up at the Lodge was almost all handwork—there was only one team of horses that was used on the job—it was Charley Maki's team from Copper Harbor—'Nick' and 'Dick'—run by Charley's adopted son, Wesley. We—Clarence Chaput and I—cut the logs for the cabin out of the woods that paralleled Aetna Creek. Wesley would work up on the golf course project all day and then, at the end of the day—before he brought the team back to Copper Harbor, he'd load up our logs—the logs that Clarence and I had cut that day—and haul them down to our building site on the harbor."

Martin continued, "The thing was, the team always had trouble getting up the hill on 41 from Aetna Creek—the hill that the golf course is on above Aetna Creek Swamp—the hill that starts its rise just about where that first 'Keweenaw Mountain Lodge' sign is (i.e., the first sign encountered when one is coming from Lake Medora). As you might imagine, by the end of the day those horses were tired—they had, after all, worked all day up at the golf course. Well, Wesley would just beat the bejesus out of Nick and Dick to get them up and over that hill. Here it is—what—65 years later and I can still recall the crack of Wesley's whip and remember how bad I felt for those horses. Once they got up the hill, it was okay—from there it was all downhill into Copper Harbor—but getting up that hill, that was the problem."

Beginning of work on cottages, probably January-February, 1936.

Cottage construction, March, 1936. Ridgeline of West Bluff (Brockway Mountain Drive) is evident in background of photograph. Note use of hand-crafted scaffolding.

Enclosing the lower level of the Clubhouse, spring, 1936. Note WPA sign mounted on tree.

Spring, 1934 found the fairways cleared and the design of the golf course finalized. Fairway seeding, which had started in early May, was completed during the summer. On Sunday, August 27, 1934, the first green was seeded; by the end of that week seeding of the remaining greens and tees was completed.

During the summer of 1934, a small log dam was built on the west side of US 41 to contain Aetna Creek. A pump and a 3" water line was installed to convey the impounded water about a third of a mile from the dam to a small pond located at the foot of number six green, the pond being designed into the golf course plan as a water hazard. A pump house was constructed adjacent to the pond to distribute the water around the nine hole course.

Ocha Potter—one-time club champion at the Calumet Golf Course—was intimately involved in the design of the Keweenaw Park golf course and is generally credited as its architect. That said, KCRC records indicate that at least several other individuals were instrumental in developing the golf course plan. Notably, KCRC Surveyor, Harry A. Swanson, drafted the layout and engineered the physical design of the course. Additionally, November 17, 1933, KCRC Board minutes are explicit in the authorization of the payment of "up to $200 for an expert in golf course design."

Longtime Copper Harbor summer resident Mary Macdonald—an avid golfer and friend of the Potter family—recalled in a late 1980s interview that, "a golf pro was brought in from down around the Escanaba-Iron Mountain area to design the course." Beyond that recollection, however, Macdonald was unable to name or otherwise identify who was brought in. Accordingly, what appears most probable is that the design of the Keweenaw Park golf course was not an accomplishment by just one person, but rather, an achievement stemming from the efforts and contributions of several individuals.

The final design for the Keweenaw Park course called for the first nine holes to be a par 36 and to have a distance of 3,240 yards. The layout of the second nine holes—the course which was never completed—was similarly planned to be a par 36, with a distance of 3,319 yards. The complete 72 par course, had it been constructed, would have been the first 18 hole golf course built in the Upper Peninsula.

Ocha Potter Leaves the Project:

In summer, 1934, Ocha Potter was involuntarily removed from any direct responsibility for the Keweenaw Park and Golf Course project. Several years later Potter wrote his autobiography, *Sixty Years*, an unpublished work in which he expressed his opinions and viewpoints relative to the circumstances encompassing his termination:

> "Then federal and state officials began to interfere. Professional social workers were constantly investigating and unconsciously stirring opposition. Speeches from the White House caused class prejudice to rear its ugly head. Soon there were mutterings that golf was a rich man's game and the sentiment spread that advantage was being taken of the working man's misfortune to provide a play ground for the wealthy. Broken by over work and nerve strain, I resigned from all relief work in mid-February 1934 and went on a months auto tour to California taking advantage of the trip to study famous golf courses and tourist resorts. Upon my return I agreed upon the request of state officials to again take charge of relief work.... But by this time continuous propaganda had ripened its fruit. The men refused to work on the golf course and went on strike with the usual daily parades and of course, a lavish display of the U.S. flag. Have you ever faced 350 angry

Michigan College of Mining and Technology Alumni Reunion, August, 7, 1936. Note that in this photograph, while the porch is open, the lower level or "basement" has been enclosed.

View of west side of Clubhouse, probably about 1937–38.

men—alone? Well, I have. And it isn't pleasant. State and federal relief officials—professional social workers and politicians—came to investigate. They listened to the complaints with sympathetic ears and a compromise was soon reached whereby the work at the golf course and club house would be carried on on a restricted basis with the provision that I should be eliminated. I was asked to resign, refused and was promptly discharged from responsibilities I had carried on more than two years as a volunteer. Paid professional social workers took my place and our people became 'clients'."

Potter was and—to this day—remains a controversial figure. He was a "doer"—a "go getter"—an energetic and dominant individual who, in his role as Superintendent of the Ahmeek Mining Company, was a powerful figure in Keweenaw County. Yet, it is also clear that Potter was not a personality who was especially well liked. To the contrary, there would be no winning of any popularity contests by the likes of Ocha Potter.

It must have been humiliating for Ocha Potter—an authoritative figure—an individual with a commanding presence—to be "discharged" from the Keweenaw Park and Golf Course project. In this regard, it may be that Potter's autobiographical assessment constitutes a case of self-justification—a face-saving rationalization—to reconcile his termination. This is especially so when one considers that there is no evidence that there was ever any type of a strike, slowdown, or other type of labor demonstration that ever occurred at the Keweenaw Park work site.

Should the "strikes" and "daily parades" mentioned in Potter's recollections actually have occurred—as regularly as Potter implies—there should be at least some mention of them in local newspapers. To the contrary, a review of Houghton's *Daily Mining Gazette*, Hancock's *Evening Copper Journal*, and Calumet's *Calumet News*, failed to find any evidence—not even a single mention—of any work stoppage, slowdown, "parade" or other labor demonstration at the work site.

Historical dialogues in the 1990s with the likes of Howard Bergh, Al Long, and Walter Riistola, all of whom were employed on the Keweenaw Park and Golf Course job site during the first years of the project, were remarkable in that they confirmed the absence of any worksite labor unrest. As Riistola commented, "We were happy—no, actually, we were thrilled—to be working. As long as I live, I'll never forget Christmas, 1933—it was the first time in a long time that I actually had enough money to be able to buy Christmas gifts. In terms of the work, the only problem that ever came up was transportation to and from the job. We had to ride back and forth in the back of dump trucks—I'll tell you, it was cold and miserable. I don't think (KCRC Engineer Wm. C. "Clem") Veale really cared how we got out there as long as the work got done. Eventually, Victor Oja—he was the Road Commission's Superintendent for the golf course job—interceded with Veale and they rented some buses from

Northeastern view of Clubhouse and horizon. Photo taken from the catwalk of Keweenaw Park's elevated water tank. Lake Superior, Porter's Island and Copper Harbor lighthouse are all visible in distance. The newly constructed tennis court is visible in photograph; accordingly, image likely dates to about 1937–38.

Photograph of cottages, 1938. Cottage number 1 is located in right foreground of image. There is an anteroom attached to the backside of number 1 cottage in this photograph; this portion of the structure would be removed in a later remodeling of the cottage.

Copper Range Company to transport us. Of course, with the buses coming from Copper Range, we heard through the grapevine that that then created another problem—some of the big shots in the county didn't like that—the north end of the Keweenaw was Calumet and Hecla territory."

In a similar vein, Copper City resident Hank Pellikka observed that while there were intermittent labor troubles which marked both the FERA and WPA programs, such never occurred up on the Keweenaw Park worksite. According to Pellikka, "…there were marches in the Mohawk area protesting WPA working conditions—too much work and too little pay and so forth. They would march from the Mohawk school—at the time there was a large bank building on that corner—over to the Ahmeek Fire Hall. Mike Stefanich—he's dead now—was the flag carrier and one of the rabble rousers. It happened a couple of times on a couple of weekends and then it was over."

Pellikka elaborated, "My bet is that Potter got himself into trouble politically—in those days all the bosses were Republicans and almost all the workers were Democrats—and when Roosevelt and his supporters got in, they cleaned house. I remember that there was a district WPA Administrator by the name of Hook—he took his politics seriously—and he could be a holy terror if you weren't on the right side politically."

Potter would continue to be tangentially involved in the Keweenaw Park and Golf Course project as a member of the Keweenaw County Road Commission—and correspondingly—as a member of the Keweenaw County Board of Park Trustees. While Potter was not reappointed to serve on these boards for the 1937–39 period (the direct election of Keweenaw County Road Commissioners did not begin until 1976), he was, in 1939, after a two year hiatus, renamed to the governing bodies. Potter was appointed Chairman of KCRC (and the Keweenaw County Board of Park Trustees) in 1944; he continued to serve on these authorities until 1950.

Regardless of the accuracy of Ocha Potter's reminiscences, it was he who, more than most, recognized the decline—and inevitable end—of copper mining in the Keweenaw. An early and influential advocate for the development of regional tourism, it is Ocha Potter who must be credited with originating the idea and laying the groundwork which led to the Keweenaw Park and Golf Course project.

THE CLUBHOUSE

The Keweenaw Park and Golf Course Clubhouse was designed by the Engineering Department of Calumet and Hecla, with the company donating the cost of their architectural and engineering services. The design drew inspiration from the Shingle, Bungalow, and Western Stick architectural styles of the early 1900s and reflected connections to the Arts and Crafts Movement. The resulting rustic log design came to resemble the camp architecture popular at the turn of the century. Similar designs—sometimes referred to by the whimsical term "parkitecture"—are often encountered in the wilderness resort areas of New York's Adirondack Mountains and the Western Region parks of the U. S. National Park System.

The Clubhouse was designed as a 96 foot x 59 foot hall built of precisely fitted and grooved log walls with a low-pitched gable roof, open at the sides and dormers. As originally constructed, the broadly pitched roof slope continued

View towards west of Clubhouse porch and main entrance, about 1935–36. Through the Clubhouse's main entranceway would have been what Stan Martin referred to as "the imposing solid log wall—with the hole in the wall," with regular-sized entrance doors located perpendicularly on either side of the wall.

View towards east of recently enclosed Clubhouse porch and main entrance, 1939-40. The location of this photograph was later the site of the bar and is now the location of the management and administrative offices. Note copper chandeliers, the same crafted in Calumet & Hecla's metal shop.

Southern view of west side of Clubhouse porch, about 1935-36. Note rustic furniture, handcrafted by Lauri Linna and KCRC work crew during the winter of 1934-35.

around the front, back and sides and covered an open, gallery-like, porch. The open porch consisted of log supports and balustrade in an open-work pattern of diagonal and horizontal log railings. An additional perpendicular roof formed a canopied entrance in the center of the front façade. The exterior of the structure combined native wood and stone to create a visually appealing building which blended naturally with the northern landscape.

The interior of the Clubhouse was accentuated by openly displayed structural details, including exposed beams and rafters. The east half of the structure was designed to contain a dining room and the west half, a lounge and bar. Each end of the building was accented by a massive, uncoursed, rough cut, stone masonry fireplace. Originally, the Clubhouse contained a second-story loft area; accessed by an unskirted wooden stairway, the loft area was used for a number of summers as a residence by the Keweenaw Park's then full-time golf professional, Al Bovard.

As documented in a June, 1934 letter from Keweenaw County to the State Emergency Relief Administration office, the start of work on the Clubhouse was delayed because of the inability of the County to locate a suitable professional to supervise the construction phase of the project. This was resolved by the appointment of KCRC Engineer Wm. C. "Clem" Veale as Keweenaw Park Construction Manager and KCRC Foreman Victor Oja as on-site Construction Superintendent.

Craftsmen and working foremen of note on the summer, 1934 building project included Ed Ackley and Silas Remillard who led construction of the log framework. Louis Azzi, an Italian mason, designed and built the fireplaces and chimneys.

By late fall, 1934 the basic structure was complete. Finishing details included hammered copper chandeliers and light fixtures, which are still in use today and were made in Calumet & Hecla's Metal Shop. Fireplace screens, also still in use today, were made in the Keweenaw County Road Commission shop. During the ensuing winter carpentry crews, led by master craftsman Lauri Linna, fabricated log furniture for use in the Clubhouse dining and lounge areas; although since replaced, this represented a practical use of existing resources and continued the rustic motif.

Northern view of recently enclosed west side Clubhouse porch, 1939–40. The room depicted in the background of this photograph—the northwest corner of the Clubhouse—would be remodeled in future years, serving first as a bar area for the lounge, and in later years, as the location of the Manager's office.

Main dining room, about 1935–36

Lounge and bar area, about 1935–36. Metal fireplace screens were crafted by the Keweenaw County Road Commission shop.

Stan Martin recalled "checking out" the Clubhouse structure during the summer of 1934, as it was undergoing construction: "I remember walking in from the west side—the west log wall was up about as far as my waist—and most of the north wall was up. The structural members for the roof were not up yet—you could look right up and through the roof area and all you could see was blue sky. There certainly wasn't much there, but nevertheless, there was enough there that you could tell that when it was done, it was going to be an impressive structure."

Martin continued: "What was ironic was that when the Clubhouse opened, it was truly an imposing building—with a grand entrance—and then you'd walk inside and run smack-dab into an imposing solid log wall. Back in those days the porch was open and where the main entrance hallway is now—just past today's reception desk area—there was a solid log wall. There was a hole in the wall—a small window—and people would go up to the window to make dinner reservations, get their cabin reservations or gain entry to the lounge and bar—prohibition, of course, had ended just a few years prior to this. There were regular-sized doors to the left and right sides of the "hole in the wall" and you'd go though the door to the left for a meal and the door to the right for a drink. It was a crazy set-up and it certainly wasn't very inviting. That soon changed though—within a few years there was a major upgrading of the Clubhouse—and the solid log wall with the "hole in the wall" was one of the first things to go."

Opening Day—Sunday, June 23, 1935:

By Memorial Day, 1935, finishing touches to the Clubhouse, surrounding grounds and golf course were well underway.

The June 8, 1935, edition of the *Evening Copper Journal* reported that an opening day celebration at the Keweenaw Park Resort would be held on Sunday, June 23, 1935. According to the newspaper, "Work is progressing rapidly…tee markers, distance markers and flag poles were set up this past week…and a terrace is under construction at the clubhouse which will add greatly to the appearance. Special golf course score cards have been received—they have been designed to make them both a score card and an attractive advertisement of 'Keweenaw Land'—and are of size suitable for mailing in an ordinary envelope." The publication advised readers that, prior to the opening day ceremonies, the general public was invited by the Keweenaw Park Commission to visit the club house and golf course on Saturday afternoons and Sundays.

Ideal weather conditions greeted the more than 2,000 visitors who attended the Sunday, June 23rd grand opening celebration. Opening day events commenced at 12 noon, with U. W. Tervo, Keweenaw County Relief Administrator, officiating. With a uniformed color guard in attendance from the Clyde Johnson American Legion Post, Mohawk, Tervo delivered an address to the assembled. He commented, "to the sponsors, the road and park commissions, the engineers, the board of supervisors and other interested parties, this is the actual fulfillment of a dream long envisioned. To the men and women who were responsible, it is a monument to what could be done. To the people of Keweenaw County, it is the dawn of a new industry—the tourist industry—and provides a wonderful opportunity for the future."

The *Daily Mining Gazette* reported that, "then, at a signal from Tervo, the Keweenaw Band, under the direction of Wesley Williams, began playing the "Star Spangled Banner." With everybody at attention, the flag was raised—and as the crowd watched the flag rise to the top of the pole and unfurl in the breeze—Mr. Tervo announced the formal opening of the club."

Exterior view of Clubhouse and newly enclosed porch area, about 1939. Note the center chimney protruding from the roof line in this photograph. Made of brick, the chimney vented the ovens used in the Clubhouse's earliest kitchen, as well as a heating unit located in the second-story residential loft. In a subsequent remodeling, the chimney was removed.

Opening day entertainment included presentation of the Keweenaw Supervisors Cup. Open to any eligible amateur golfer belonging to any golf club in the U.P., the Keweenaw Supervisors Cup was established with the intention that it would be an annual prize, one which would be awarded to the winner of the Keweenaw Park's opening day golf tournament, as held each year on a date fixed by the Keweenaw Park Commission. Won for the first time by Michigan Tech student Whiteman Brown, runners-up included Dr. C. W. Messinger, William Longacre, and Weldon LaBine, all of Houghton, and Leslie C. McClelland of Calumet. Additional opening day golf prizes were provided to participants by merchants Ed Haas & Co., Vertin Brothers Co., Carlton Hardware Co, Keckonen Hardware Co., Cloverland Picture Shop, Metropolitan Pharmacy, Johnson Vivian Jr. & Co. Store, Laurium Pharmacy, and Superior Pharmacy.

T. P. Cook of the Marquette Golf Club and Mr. Flora of the Portage Lake Golf Club were the professional golfers registered for the opening day festivities. According to the June 24, 1935, *Daily Mining Gazette*, "Mr. Flora declared that the Keweenaw course will, in no doubt, become one of the most popular in the middlewest, not only for its great scenic and natural beauty, but also for the ideal playing conditions it provides for every class of golfer. The course, Mr. Flora said, is not a difficult one, but offers many features to test the ability and ingenuity of the expert, as well as the beginner and average golfer. Mr. Cook also praised the course and its designers and declared it to be one of the best and most attractive he has ever played."

An opening day celebratory lunch was available to participants in the Clubhouse, while dinner—given what at the time were limited Clubhouse kitchen facilities—was served from 5 PM to 8 PM at the Pontiac Hotel in Copper Harbor for 85 cents a plate.

Three days later—Wednesday, June 26—a "Ladies' Day" event was held to inaugurate the facility. Featuring a golf and bridge tournament for ladies only, the occasion was led and managed by a group of nearly 100 women, self-organized into committees handling arrangements for transportation, golf, bridge, prizes, entertainment, and refreshments. The "Ladies' Day" committee constituted a veritable economic and social "who's who" of Keweenaw and northern Houghton County, counting among its membership individuals such as Mrs. Chas. A. Wright, Mrs. H. S. Goodell, Mrs. Norman Macdonald, Mrs. Frank Carlton, Mrs. Peter Ruppe, Mrs. A. C. Roche, Mrs. A. E. Petermann, Mrs. C. H. Benedict, Mrs. Leslie McClelland, Mrs. E. P. Lovell, Mrs. W. F. Hartmann, Mrs. Charles Lawton, Mrs. Austin Raley, Mrs. Michael Foley, Mrs. Herman Gundlach, Mrs. Harry Vivian, and Mrs. W. C. Veale.

The cost of the Keweenaw Park and Golf Course project, as reported by Louis M. Nims, Work Division Director for the State Emergency Relief Administration, was $146,092. However, the 167 acres of land contributed by the Keweenaw Copper Company was considered to have a value of $20,000, reducing the actual financial cost of the project to $126,092. Similar to other Depression-era work relief propositions, about 75% of all expenditures went to pay wages, with the remaining 25% being dispensed in payment for goods, materials and miscellaneous services. Apparently, the majority of the work—and the majority of the funds—went into the golf course portion of the project. This is indirectly confirmed by KCRC Board minutes of October 12, 1934, which authorized the "insuring of the Golf Course Clubhouse and contents for not less than $25,000."

The first season of operation—from the Sunday, June 23rd Opening Day celebration, through the last day of operation, Sunday, September 15th—marked the start of a popular and successful resort facility. Indeed, by the end of the first summer, the Keweenaw Park Clubhouse had become THE spot to "see and be seen" in Keweenaw County. And if comments from out of area visitors were any indication, the resort was well on its way to achieving the goal of boosting the regional economy through tourism:

From Grand Rapids: "My only regret is that Grand Rapids is so far away from the Keweenaw."
From Milwaukee: "I am coming up again."
From Pittsburgh, Penn.: "I think the set up is perfect and will be a big help in attracting tourists—the Copper Country's next industry."
From Okmulgee, Okla.: "Nothing like it in Oklahoma."
From Chicago: "Wonderful, superb, beautiful."

Northern view of recently enclosed west side Clubhouse porch, 1939–40. The room depicted in the background of this photograph—the northwest corner of the Clubhouse—would be remodeled in future years, serving first as a bar area for the lounge, and in later years, as the location of the Manager's office.

Photograph of Keweenaw Park's flower gardens, about 1941–42.

Keweenaw Park wait staff standing in garden area. Mid 1940s.

THE W.P.A. ERA-EXPANSION AND EVOLUTION

The Federal Emergency Relief Administration program (FERA), was replaced in 1935 by the Works Progress Administration—the WPA—which was renamed in 1939 the Works Projects Administration. WPA expanded upon the offerings of the earlier FERA agency. Nationally, the WPA program employed millions to carry out public works projects, including the construction of public buildings, roads and bridges, the operation of arts, drama and literary projects and the distribution of food, clothing and housing. Until ended by Congress in 1943, amid the employment boom caused by WW II, WPA was both the largest New Deal agency and the largest employer in the United States.

In terms of the Keweenaw Park and Golf Course undertaking, the November 30, 1935 minutes of the Keweenaw County Road Commission document the efforts of local officials to obtain WPA support for continued development of the resort project: "The WPA program was discussed at length and plans for employing the men were formulated. It was decided to urge the WPA office in Iron Mountain to do everything possible to further the cottage project, road project and coffee shop improvements and all other projects turned in by the Road Commission."

What resulted was the WPA assuming a prominent role in the continued development of the Keweenaw Park and Golf Course project. Starting in January, 1936 and continuing through the early 1940s, the WPA bankrolled a series of enhancements and upgrades to the facility. These improvements, which included the following separate projects, served to transform the resort into a popular tourist destination: 1) Cottages; 2) Clubhouse Foundation Enclosure and "Shantytown" Construction; 3) Recreation; 4) Infrastructure; and, 5) 1939 Clubhouse Remodeling.

Cottages:

Cy Clark replaced Bill Bolley as a member of the Keweenaw County Road Commission in September, 1935. More than any other individual, it was Clark who moved the "Cottages" project forward, enabling it to obtain WPA funding.

The Cottages project initially entailed building eight log cabin-style rental units (i.e., today's cottages 1 though 8) along the fairway side of the golf course. The units, of either single or duplex style, were designed by KCRC staffers Harry Swanson and Art Hagman.

Cottage construction began in January, 1936. All structures were approximately 25 x 30 feet in size, with 6/12 pitch side opening gable roofs, open gable-roofed entrance porches or shed roofed side entrances, exposed or interior chimneys and large, eight paned casement windows. The structures were built of pine and cedar grooved, fitted logs. The logs were spiked together and sealed with oakum jute caulking. The floors rested on sills supported by rough coursed stone pylons. Exposed joints, rafters, exterior log railings, and gable supports formed an architectural motif which resembled the design of the Clubhouse.

Construction of seven additional log rental cottages (for a total of 15 cottages) commenced in the fall of 1935. Five of this series of structures (i.e., today's cottages nine through 14—there being no number 13) were located on the fairway side of the golf course, while the remaining two units (i.e., today's units 15 and 16) were placed on the north side of the main entrance road. The units were designed to be indistinguishable from the first eight log cottages.

Exterior of west side of Clubhouse and outside lounge area. About 1941–42.

Ten cottages were finished by July 1, 1937, with units 2 through 10 being available for rent. (During the first decades of operation of the resort, Cottage No. 1 was reserved for use by the Manager as a summer residence). Cottages 11, 12 and 14 were equipped and available for occupancy on July 15th and cottages 15 and 16 starting on September 1, 1937.

Another five cottages (for a total of 20 cottages) were built starting in late 1938 and became available for occupancy starting with the 1940 tourist season. The total cost for constructing all 20 cottages was $72,460; an average cost of $3,623 per cottage.

The addition of the cottages changed the character of the resort and prompted a facility name change. KCRC Board minutes for December 11, 1936 indicate that it was "moved and supported (and passed) that the golf course and surrounding grounds be named 'Keweenaw Park' and the cottages on the premises be called 'Keweenaw Park Cottages'..." The new name—"Keweenaw Park and Cottages"—was featured in a full page advertisement in the 1937 Keweenaw Vacationist League brochure.

Evidently, the construction of so many rental units—in such a relatively short period of time—engendered a backlash from area entrepreneurs. KCRC Board minutes of March 10, 1939, indicated that, "Whereas it has come to the attention of the Keweenaw County Road Commission that there is a general impression that it is the purpose or plan of this Commission to enlarge or expand the tourist accommodations of Keweenaw County in competition with private capital providing similar accommodations, and, Whereas, it is the real purpose and desire of this Commission to encourage the profitable and suitable development of the tourist resources of this County, BE IT RESOLVED, that this Commission go on record as being opposed to the building or erection of any additional housing accommodations for tourists in excess of the cottages and cabins now nearing completion."

Clubhouse Foundation Enclosure and "Shantytown" Construction:

Winter, 1936—in addition to the Cottages Project—marked the start of WPA financed projects to 1) enclose the foundation or lower level of the Clubhouse, and 2) construct employee housing, what became known as "Shantytown."

Enclosure of the Clubhouse foundation enabled a portion of the basement area to be used as both a coffee shop and site of shower and locker room facilities. This area would be remodeled a second time, in 1939. In the interim, the area provided a spot for both golfers and employees—especially employees living in "Shantytown"—to eat and wash up.

"Shantytown" was built in 1936 and was a collection of 13 small, approximately 8 foot x 10 foot, wooden shacks. Located in the field east of the tennis court, the bungalows contained bunk beds and were intended to provide resident

Photograph of Keweenaw Park bear feeding station. Probably mid 1940s.

Cottages, winter, about 1941–42. Note depth of snow relative to bottom of cottage window sills.

One of the last surviving "Shantytown" cabins. September 6, 2009.

employees with summer living quarters. The huts were heated by small wood stoves (some of the shacks also had plug-in electrical heaters) and were illuminated by a single, bare, incandescent bulb which hung down from the center of room. One of the centrally located shacks was plumbed, serving as a toilet building, with cold running water. Employees—generally high school and college-age waitresses, "cabin boys," "cabin girls," and golf caddies—needed to walk over to the Clubhouse basement for meals or to shower.

Bill Clark, a resident of Marquette and Great Sand Bay, worked at Keweenaw Park—and lived in Shantytown—the summers of 1937, 1938 and part of the summer of 1939. Clark recollected: "We lived 3 to 4 in a cabin—the girls in some and the boys in the others. It was a fun place—we really had a good time. We were paid $20 a month, plus room and board, plus whatever we could pick up in tips. We were glad to have the job. In fact, you had to know someone to even get the job. (Bill Clark's father, Cy Clark, was a KCRC board member, and starting in 1939, was KCRC Chairman). Everyone lived off of the tips, but in those days, people didn't tip much—times were tough. I was a Cabin Boy—a glorified Bell Hop—and did okay—generally though, the girls did better than the boys in the tip department."

Clark elaborated: "What was interesting was that just about everyone who golfed was from down around Calumet and Houghton—they were all doctors, lawyers and business executives. Of course, at the time, golf was considered to be a rich man's game—poor people didn't play golf in those days. There were a few folks from Keweenaw County who golfed—Mrs. Veale, Perk Vivian and Dr. Bryant—but that was about it. Ocha Potter, from Ahmeek, golfed, however, I don't think I ever saw him up there—not once in the three years I was there. Clem Veale was there all the time—(and as Clark commented with a chuckle in his voice)—I don't think he ever paid for a drink or a meal—not once. Having the golf course there, though, I think what it did was to prompt people in Keweenaw County to take the game up."

Recreation:

WPA funded recreational pursuits at Keweenaw Park included a horseshoe pit, a tennis court, a shuffle board court, a "Greens Shack" (today's Pro Shop, which cost $4,493 to erect in 1936), a barn for saddle horses, and the 1940 construction of a concrete platform to be used as a "bear feeding ground" (located

Portion of Keweenaw Park and Cabins rate card and brochure, 1940.

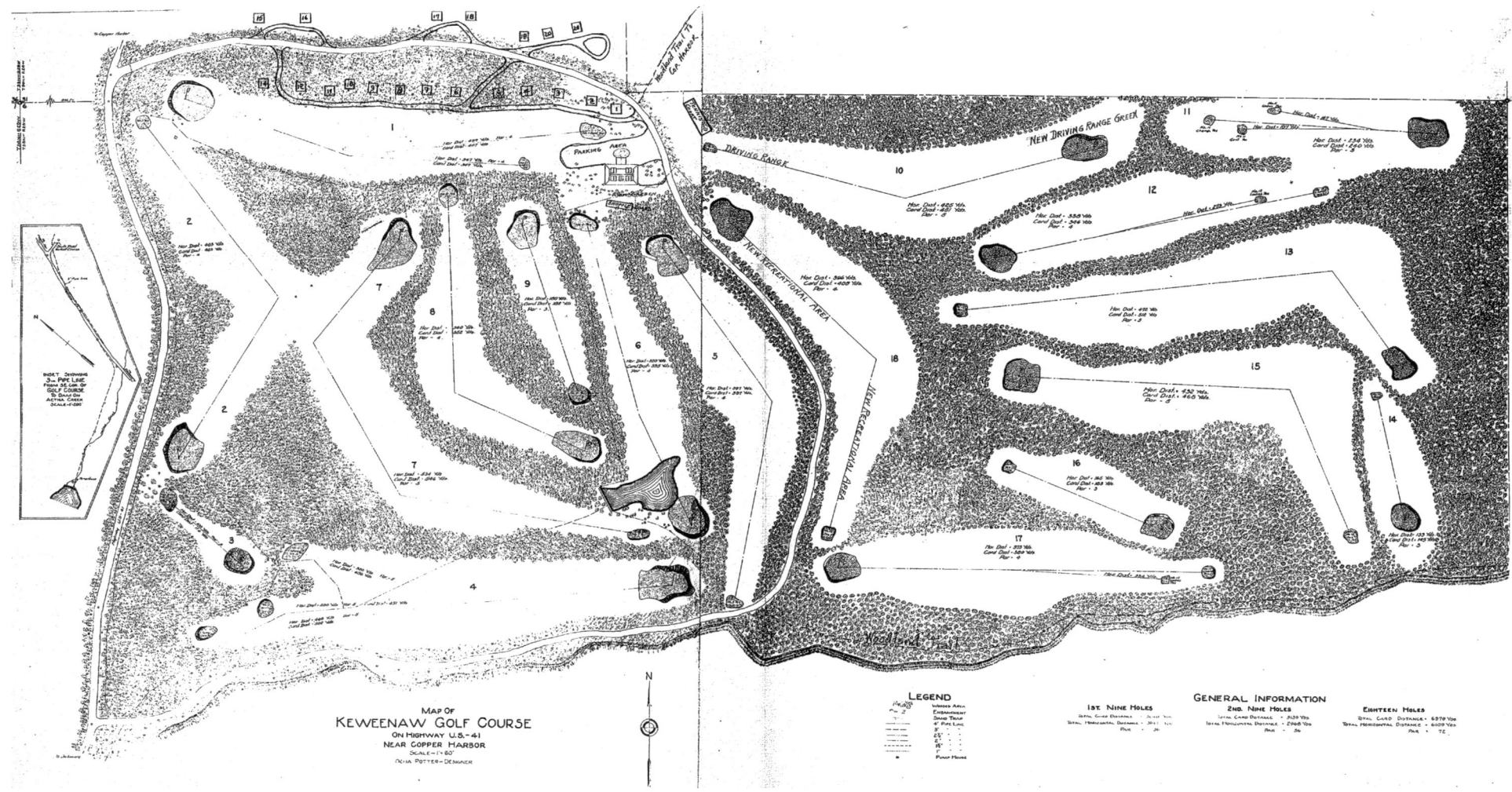

KCRC composite drawing of plan for 18 hole golf course at Keweenaw Park, 1934. Drawing later modified to show addition of cottages, driving range, etc.

directly across US 41 from the main entrance gate). Additionally, the National Youth Administration—the WPA's junior division—constructed two "woodland hiking trails," one between the resort and Copper Harbor, with the other running from the south side of the golf course to Lake Manganese.

Annually, WPA picked up the costs of golf course fairway improvements, especially the covering of bare spots and rock ledges with additional soil, and the seeding of these areas. From the start of the golf course project, there was very little soil covering the fairways, with the situation being compounded by conglomerate formations outcropping at the surface. Much of the grass seed, when planted, did not germinate, resulting in large bare areas on all of the fairways. The only remedy for this condition was to, on an annual basis, bring in soil and cover the fairway bare spots with earth, reseeding as necessary.

On at least three different occasions, WPA rejected proposals to finance completion of the second nine holes of the golf course. After rejecting, for the third

View of the front of a "fairway side cottage" as seen from the main entrance road.

View of cottages #1 and #2; ridgeline of Brockway Mountain Drive is visible in background. About 1937–38.

time, the finishing of the second nine holes, the WPA did consent to fund construction of a golf driving range. Built on the site of the No. 10 fairway, the project was viewed as a means of removing one of the scars—which was visually apparent from the main entrance to the Clubhouse—resulting from the roughing out of the second nine holes of the originally proposed 18 hole course.

Other recreational project proposals submitted to WPA, which were rejected by the government agency, included: 1) Construction of an outdoor swimming pool; 2) A proposal to purchase land at the end of Lake Medora for use as a bathing beach; 3) A proposition to purchase saddle horses and build 20 miles of saddle horse trails, including construction of eight trailside shelters; and 4) Demolition of the existing "Greens Shack,"—today's Pro Shop—replacing it with an expanded building, which would have included men's and women's shower and locker facilities, as well as a bar and grill.

Following WPA's turn down of the swimming pool and bathing beach concepts, KCRC asked Keweenaw Copper Company to donate a Lake Medora beach parcel to the Park; apparently, nothing ever materialized from the overture. After having the "saddle horse and trail" plan declined by WPA, KCRC, in 1938, entered into a contract permitting U. R. Warjakka of Mohawk to provide mounts to the tourists at Keweenaw Park.

Lastly, there was one recreational project which was submitted to—and approved by—WPA, but which was never built. This proposal entailed the construction of an archery and trap shooting range. Submitted in 1941 and approved for the 1942 season, the project was suspended—and later cancelled—because of the entrance of the United States into World War II.

Infrastructure:

Infrastructure projects, including the construction of water and electrical systems were, in financial terms, the second largest subset of Keweenaw Park projects funded by WPA. The sum of $61,083 was advanced by WPA in 1938 for work which modified the existing water system and which tied the resort into the Houghton County Electric Light Company (predecessor to Upper Peninsula Power Company—UPPCO) power distribution grid.

The water system modification was prompted by inconsistent flow from Aetna Creek. The 1938 project involved removing and salvaging the 3" water line which had previously connected the resort to Aetna Creek Dam. The line was then re-laid and extended—running a total of 7,300 feet—to connect with a 30 HP pump constructed at the foot of 3rd Street in Copper Harbor. The project included the construction of a 10,000 gallon, 18' elevated steel water storage tank at Keweenaw Park. The newly installed system entailed a 538.4 foot elevation rise from the level of Lake Superior to the top of the tank at Keweenaw Park.

Bill Clark recalled the water system installation: "They bought the tank—used—out of Toivola. Back in those days they used everything over again—nothing went to waste. It was kind of funny—in the course of transporting the tank from Toivola to Copper Harbor, they had to cross the old Portage Lake Bridge—the swing bridge—and darned if in the process of crossing it, they didn't knock just about every light right off the bridge."

The original elevated water storage tank (replaced in the 1999–2000 era) had a wooden catwalk around the elevated base of the tank; it was accessed from the ground by a wooden stairway. Throughout the 1930s and 1940s, the water tank catwalk was a popular spot for tourists and visitors to use as an observation platform. The spot—until the surrounding trees grew up—was one from which the Copper Harbor Lighthouse and passing freighters on Lake Superior could be viewed.

When the Clubhouse opened in 1935, Phoenix was the nearest location where it was possible to connect to the electric power grid, prompting KCRC to purchase and install a Kohler electrical generating plant at Keweenaw Park. Then, in 1936, under the auspices of a different WPA project, electric utility lines were run from Phoenix to Eagle Harbor.

Two years later—in 1938—WPA approved a project to extend the electric utility lines from Eagle Harbor to Keweenaw Park, via Copper Harbor. Stretching for 16 miles, the lines generally ran alongside state highway M-26, partially following the path of what had been the U. S. Coast Guard's Eagle Harbor to Manitou Island (telephone) "pole line." Costing $24,638 to install, much of the work centered on the cutting, framing and erecting of 30–35 foot high utility poles. (The USCG poles had been 20 feet tall and were of insufficient height to safely carry high voltage electrical current).

The electrical project tied the Village of Copper Harbor into the Houghton County Electric Light Company power distribution system. Interestingly, Copper Harbor's electrical usage soon skyrocketed. Within a few years, Keweenaw Park began to experience electrical "brown outs," prompting KCRC to take the stand, in a May, 1941, communication, that "while Copper Harbor's use of electricity is steadily increasing…Keweenaw Park has and reserves prior use of the line."

Another infrastructure improvement funded by the WPA included the fall, 1940, construction of nearly 2,000 feet of rough cut stone walls—what were designated in engineering documents as "rubble post guard rails"—bordering the US 41 boundary of the property. This work was done under the supervision of stone mason Swanee Maki and coincided with the first hard surfacing of US 41. Shortly thereafter, the Clubhouse entranceway was upgraded, adding cobblestone steps and decorative urns.

In terms of other infrastructure projects, WPA refused a 1935 request to fund erection of a 13 mile telephone line, from Delaware to Keweenaw Park. The proposed line was to have been extended to Copper Harbor and from there to Fort Wilkins State Park. WPA, in declining the request, indicated that the project was "outside the scope of WPA authorizations." (Within a few years, a telephone line would be strung alongside the 1938 Eagle Harbor-Copper Harbor-Keweenaw Park electric utility line. Prior to that time, reservations for a stay at Keweenaw Park had to be made by mail or telephoned or wired into KCRC's main office—then located in Ahmeek—with the reservation subsequently being "hand carried" out to Keweenaw Park.)

Possibly the most audacious local project proposed to—and declined by—WPA involved construction of an airport at Copper Harbor. Dated March 23, 1942, the request contemplated building an "air transportation landing field" on the south side of Copper Harbor, on the site of the Wescoat farm. The rationale for the request included the justification that, in addition to supporting the war effort, it would help "encourage regional tourism, providing ready access to Keweenaw Park and Cottages."

View of new tennis court, a 1936 WPA project.

1939 Clubhouse Remodeling:

Remodeling of the Clubhouse was the principal WPA funded construction project carried out at Keweenaw Park in 1939. The work included enclosure of the formerly open porch, expansion of the kitchen, and upgrading of the lower level—what is sometimes called the "basement."

When the Clubhouse was designed, it was thought that the building would function primarily as a daytime facility, operating mostly as an adjunct to the golf course, typically on a "dawn to dusk" schedule. Based on the premise that it would most likely serve only a limited number of meals—and at that, mostly light meals and lunches—the Clubhouse was designed with a small kitchen.

The need to feed more people on more of a varied schedule was largely a consequence of the success which the resort had experienced since its opening four years earlier. Both the addition of the cottages (which did not contain kitchens) and the ever increasing popularity of Keweenaw Park brought forward the need to expand the Clubhouse's food preparation and dining capabilities.

The kitchen remodeling phase of the project entailed the construction of an L-shaped kitchen addition at the rear of the Clubhouse. Commercial food preparation equipment was purchased and installed; these changes afforded the Clubhouse the ability to provide complete and comprehensive meal preparation services, accommodating large numbers of patrons.

The porch segment of the project entailed the addition of eight-paned wooden casement windows with glass panels below, transforming the formerly open veranda into an enclosed structure. New front doors were added and the foyer was remodeled, creating a more inviting entranceway.

Several years after completion of the porch enclosure project, the dining area was moved from the east hall area to "the porch." Sofas and lounge chairs were then purchased for the vacated east hall area—the former dining room—enabling the space to be converted into a salon. Eventually, the ever increasing popularity of dining at Keweenaw Park resulted in both the porch and the east hall spaces being used as dining seating areas.

The lower level or "basement" portion of the 1939 Clubhouse remodeling project involved enlarging the substructure by blasting rock out from the area beneath the Clubhouse. This work was performed by blasters Bill Phillips and Ludwig Nordstrom, both of whom were former miners; with considerable fanfare it was noted that the work was accomplished without breaking a single window in the Clubhouse structure above. The expansion of the basement provided room for the construction of a kitchen storage area and the installation of food refrigeration equipment.

Following expansion of the lower level, a combined coffee shop-snack bar with fountain and bar service, was established in the southeast corner of the basement. Popularly called "The Grill"—and in later years, "The MacGregor Room"—the casual atmosphere of this setting quickly made it a popular alternative to the more formal ambience of the Clubhouse's main dining room.

Following completion of the 1939 Clubhouse Remodeling project, Keweenaw Park hired George Jamison as Chef; Jamison proved to be instrumental in making dining at the Clubhouse popular. Soon putting on one's "Sunday best" clothes and going up to the Clubhouse for dinner became the "thing to do" in the Copper Country.

WORLD WAR II AND POSTWAR PROSPERITY

As the 1940s began, Keweenaw Park was essentially a complete and finished project. The development of the golf course, the construction and subsequent remodeling of the Clubhouse and the completion of the cottage project all served to establish the fundamental attributes of the resort. Although alterations and revisions would occur to the facility over the course of the next 50 years, none would significantly change the basic character of the development.

Keweenaw Park helped foster the tourism potential of Michigan's Keweenaw. In the pre-World War II era, the facility maintained an ambiance of sophisticated respectability and was known for stylish attire, tasteful entertainment, and refined relations.

Bob Carlton, a resident of Lake Linden and Agate Harbor, recalled the early 1940s: "I started at Calumet High in the fall of 1939. That summer one of my friends had been a caddie up at the Keweenaw Park Golf Course and had bunked up in Shantytown. Back in those days the caddies had a uniform of sorts that they wore—it was a tan shirt with the Keweenaw Park logo monogrammed on it. My friend had several of the shirts left over after the summer ended and gave one to me. I remember wearing it around Calumet High—it was really sharp looking—I'll never forget how proud I felt the first time I put it on."

Carlton elaborated: "Back in those days the Clubhouse was absolutely immaculate—it was a first class operation—everything about the place was superbly, just impeccably, maintained. There was a bar, grill and coffee shop in the basement—and there was a fulltime bartender down there, too. The golfers were forever traipsing in and out. What I remember most though was that in those days a (deluxe) cottage at Keweenaw Park rented for $14 a day. Mind you, this was at a time when men were earning $44 a month working for WPA. To me, that amount of money—$14 for a cottage—was just astronomical."

With annual revenues averaging $70,000, Keweenaw Park had, by 1940, established itself as a popular and financially successful venture. Flush with cash, the facility helped cover general County budget shortfalls by regularly transferring excess funds into the general accounts of Keweenaw County.

Then, by summer 1942, the effects of World War II began to be felt. Unlike many resort facilities—which closed for the duration of the conflict—Keweenaw Park remained open throughout the war. It was, however, a financially challenging time for the facility. Gasoline and tire rationing resulted in a drastic reduction in the numbers of both day-use and longer-term customers. War-time price inflation had a negative influence on the cost of purchased goods, while Office of Price Administration (OPA) price controls prevented Keweenaw Park from raising its rates. What resulted was Keweenaw Park losing money from operations—for the very first time—in 1943.

The difficulty of hiring and retaining good employees was another factor which characterized operation of the resort during the war years. As Ahmeek resident Frank Stubenrauch related: "My Dad, Frank, worked up at the Lodge—he was involved in building the cabins. My Uncle Henry (Stubenrauch) worked up there too—he was Head Gardener from the time the resort first opened up until World War II, when he left for Detroit. As soon as World War II started, the Keweenaw emptied right out—just about everyone left for Detroit, some for Chicago and places like that. That's where the good jobs were—that's where the good pay was—not back in the Keweenaw."

Prosperity returned to Keweenaw Park following the end of the war. The period between 1945 and 1955 marked the high point of financial success for the resort. The post-World War II period—sometimes referred to as the "golden age of automobile-based tourism"—saw huge increases in the number of vacations taken as road trips. Families went camping in state and federal parks, sought out cultural experiences and natural resource adventures or otherwise explored the "north country." Rural country resorts such as Keweenaw Park attracted many of these visitors. That said, the characteristics of the customer base began to change as middle-class families began to frequent the resort in ever increasing numbers.

The overwhelming popularity and financial success of the cabins in the aftermath of WW II led the Park Trustees to decide, in 1946, to add four additional "duplex-type" cottages. This occurred despite the formal resolution of seven years earlier—in 1939—when, in response to pressure from local businessmen, the agency had gone on record as being opposed to the building of any additional cottages. Construction started in the spring of 1947 with the new units "fitted in" among the existing cottages on the north side of the entrance road. In today's cottage numbering system these are units 17, 18, 24, and 25. The four cottages were paid for from Keweenaw Park operating profits; costing approxicmately $40,000 to build—$10,000 a cottage—they were opened starting with the 1948 tourist season.

The addition of the last four cottages marked the culmination of the "cottages project". Today, the cottage units look identical to the way they did when first constructed, with two exceptions—Cottage 22—which burned to the ground during the 1964-70 "private ownership era"—and Cottage 6—which was destroyed by fire in 1989; this last blaze resulting in a fatality. Each of the destroyed cottages was replaced by a prefabricated log structure. Presently, Cottage 22, while it appears to be a cottage, is, in fact, a two room motel unit; Cottage 6 is a duplex handicapped accessible accommodation.

As the decade of the 1940s ended, the Keweenaw Park Board of Trustees continued to explore alternatives for further development of the resort. In the early 1950s, the Park Trustees sought funding from the Parks and Recreation Division of the Michigan Department of Conservation to, 1) finish the second nine holes of the planned 18 hole golf course, and, 2) complete construction of a sweeping, semi-circular, access road through the grounds.

Ultimately, both requests ended up being rejected by the Department of Conservation based on the fact that they were "in excess of the financial limitations of the Department's aid to local parks program." The rebuff of the request to complete the second nine holes of the golf course represented the fourth (and final) time that funding for the project was rejected by a government entity. The semi-circular access road had similarly been part of the original Keweenaw Park plan— the unused and abandoned stone entrance gate which stands today adjacent to US 41 near the southwest boundary of the golf course is a relic of this aspect of the original landscape design.

Then came the winter of 1954–1955—the first winter season that US 41 between Delaware and Copper Harbor was snow plowed. (Prior to then, wintertime highway access to Copper Harbor was via M-26—Lakeshore Drive—with that road being kept open year-round). With the Keweenaw Park grounds now being relatively accessible during the winter months, a few break-ins and several instances of vandalism occurred. Although various means of better securing the buildings and grounds were explored, none of the options studied proved to be cost effective. This eventually led to a decision by the Park Trustees to authorize the erection of telephone pole mounted lamp posts—four of them at first—commencing the dusk to dawn lighting of the Keweenaw Park grounds.

In spring, 1955, initiatives were adopted to encourage greater use of the golf course. That year, the Park Commission decided to not only maintain the existing daily rates for daily golfing, but to promote the sport by beginning the practice of issuing "golf tickets at $10 a ticket, covering eight plays." This idea would eventually lead to the adoption of today's program of selling annual golf memberships.

As the decade of the 1950s came to an end, business at Keweenaw Park began to ebb. Although the resort was still relatively profitable—the facility transferring $9,000 in profits to the Keweenaw County General Fund in 1958—the overall level of general revenues was beginning to abate.

Eagle Harbor resident Jim Boggio, who worked in the Clubhouse as 1st Bartender the summers of 1959, 1960, and 1961 reflected on the period: "The clientele was still pretty much of a group from the upper-cut of society. Some of the customers—especially from down around the Chicago area—gave us tips that were just out-of-sight."

Boggio continued. "Back in those days, the Club belonged to Clem (Veale) and he entertained lavishly. As long as I live I'll never forget the routine that we had—Clem would drive up to the front of the Clubhouse in his Oldsmobile—and as soon as he came walking in through the front door, I'd have a scotch and soda sitting on top of the bar waiting for him. Nevertheless, for those of us who were there at the time—it was apparent that times were changing—business was beginning to fall off and the Club was starting to lose money."

By the early 1960s, the prosperity associated with the postwar "golden age of automobile tourism" was coming to an end. Air travel, including inexpensive trips to the likes of warm-weather Florida, the mythical American West and far-off Europe, began to revolutionize the travel experience. The concept of a 1930s era rural resort—of simple cabins with few conveniences and a rustic nine hole golf course—began to be viewed as old fashioned and out of date. The travelling public, in their pursuit of broader and more authentic travel experiences, came to expect upgraded and expanded facilities, better services, and more amenities. In this changing business climate, it became more and more difficult for Keweenaw Park to compete for the tourist dollar.

THE PRIVATE OWNERSHIP ERA

By the time the 1960s began, the Clubhouse had reached the quarter of a century mark, with most of the rental cottages having been in service for over 20 years. Commenting on the age of the facilities, KCRC Engineer (and Keweenaw Park Manager) Clem Veale reported to the Park Trustees that, "due to the decay of the logs and the obsolescence of the buildings, the park is badly in need of repair—roofs are in need of replacement—carpets are threadbare—the cottage bathrooms are desperately in need of modernization."

Given declining revenues, however, there were hardly enough funds available to maintain the facility on a day-to-day basis—much less sufficient monies to embark upon a sustained program of modernization and upgrade.

Retired KCRC Clerk Don Zappa observed, "It always seemed as though there was lots of confusion—both on the part of the public and on the part of the Commission—between what were operating funds and what were capital funds. In my day, the Keweenaw Park business was always run on a cash basis—the Commission was only interested in making sure that cash receipts matched cash bank deposits. There was never depreciation charged against the Park's income statement, with this resulting in the reported 'profit' for the facility being artificially high. This translated into yet another problem—there was never a capital fund established to finance the long-range improvement and renovation of the facility."

With business slow and the facility losing market share, the operational focus became one of doing whatever was necessary to cut costs. Advertising in the Keweenaw Vacationist League publication was ended, and Keweenaw Park's membership in CHIA—the Copper Harbor Improvement Association—was terminated.

It was in this atmosphere that the Board of Park Trustees began an assessment and appraisal of the future of Keweenaw Park.

Focusing on such questions as the state of the facility, options for future development, funding of capital improvements and how the resort complex fit into the future of the County, a range of options was identified. These alternatives included, 1) possible sale of the resort; 2) leasing of the buildings and/or grounds to a private operator; 3) borrowing in order to fund improvements (e.g. rehabilitation of the Clubhouse and cottages, addition of a swimming pool, winterization of the Clubhouse); and 4) shortening of the summer operating season (i.e. abbreviating the season to a July 1–Labor Day schedule, from the then June 15–September 30 operating timetable).

After exploring the available alternatives, the Board of Park Trustees—in a decision endorsed by the Keweenaw County Board of Supervisors—came to the conclusion that the best option was to sell Keweenaw Park and Cottages.

At the time, Keweenaw Park had an estimated value of $225,000. However, it was unclear how much of that value could be realized through sale of the facility. Additionally, a key objective was to place the property in the hands of a party who would refurbish and winterize the complex, thus expanding employment opportunities for county residents, strengthening regional tourism.

The Park Trustees embarked upon a comprehensive marketing program to sell the facility, including advertising the availability of the property in the Wall Street Journal. As it turned out, among the critical factors influencing the eventual sale of Keweenaw Park, was a series of internal management challenges.

By way of background, Clem Veale—who, with Victor Oja, had overseen construction of the Clubhouse—and who was the first and only manager of Keweenaw Park from the time the resort was first opened—passed away Christmas morning, 1963. Veale's successor as Road Commission Engineer, John W. Jackson, had no interest in managing Keweenaw Park. Subsequently, the Park Trustees decided to split the positions of KCRC Engineer and Keweenaw Park Manager.

A new Keweenaw Park Manager, Clarence Frederick, was hired on May 8, 1964. Frederick's job performance, however, soon proved to be unacceptable. Amidst a variety of charges—including allegations that Frederick had hired his wife, placing her on the Keweenaw Park payroll as an employee and that he had regularly "exceeded his purchasing authority"—Frederick ended up being terminated less than four months later, on August 31, 1964.

Adding to the acrimonious management situation was an increasingly difficult business climate. As documented in the minutes of the September 11, 1964, meeting of the Keweenaw County Board of Park Trustees, "…the financial statements indicate that expenditures continue in excess of income…the situation is critical."

The Keweenaw County Board of Supervisors—after considering several offers—decided on November 18, 1964, to sell Keweenaw Park. Somewhat surprisingly, the Board of Park Trustees did not become aware of the Board of Supervisor's decision until the following day.

The purchasers were two Indiana residents, Merle H. Richardson and Joseph B. Quinn. The sale was structured as a land contract, with Richardson and Quinn paying $16,000 down and agreeing to pay four $16,000 installments over the next four years, for a total purchase price of $80,000.

Contractual and administrative items relating to the sale included the resolution of such issues as transfer of Keweenaw Park's liquor license, employment rights (hiring preference was to be provided first to qualified former employees, and then, to able residents of Keweenaw County), keeping Keweenaw Park open to the public (pursuant to Keweenaw Copper Company's original deed restriction, the facility and grounds were to remain open to the public in perpetuity) and disposition of the County's mineral collection (which was transferred from the Clubhouse to the County Courthouse in Eagle River).

The Richardson and Quinn partnership began operating Keweenaw Park starting with the 1965 season. The first modification made by the new owners was to change the name of the resort. The moniker Keweenaw Park was soon gone—and in its place was a new and more elegant sobriquet—Keweenaw Mountain Lodge.

As Richardson and Quinn assumed operation of the resort, the antiquated on-site employee housing facility, "Shantytown," was shut-down, with a car-pooling system (and years later, a partially subsidized van transportation system) established in its place.

Richardson and Quinn operated the Lodge for just one season. The following year the land contract with Keweenaw County was renegotiated and transferred to a new legal entity, Superior Development Corporation of Indiana. The principals of Superior Development included Granville Reynard, J. W. Watler, Charles R. Johnson, and—from the earlier ownership structure—Merle Richardson. As a condition of the new agreement with the County, Superior Development pledged to invest a minimum of $900,000 in the Lodge, modernizing the Clubhouse, installing a swimming pool, and embarking upon an extensive program of winter sports development.

Taking over operation of the Lodge at the beginning of the 1966 tourist season, Superior Development commenced construction of a full-sized swimming pool. The company replaced the original and hand-crafted—albeit antiquated—Clubhouse dining room and lounge furniture with modern furnishings and accouterments. The lounge area was remodeled, with the bar being moved from the northern side of the Clubhouse's northwest corner (the present site of the offices) to the southeast corner of the lounge.

In keeping with the times, Superior Development relaxed the rules—of some 30 years standing—as to what constituted appropriate dining room attire. The Clubhouse canon of "jacket and tie after 5," was scrapped.

Superior Development extended the Lodge's operating season, with the new schedule running from Mother's Day weekend in early May, to mid-October. Merle Richardson remained as Manager, while Herman Koldewey was brought in as Chef and maitre d'.

Despite the changes and improvements implemented by Superior Development, the organization was undercapitalized and perpetually short of cash. Within the year, the company was delinquent on the payment provided for under the terms of the sale agreement. Ultimately, in a legal action decided May 13, 1968, Circuit Judge Stephen D. Condon found Superior Development to be in default on their land contract, ruling that the company should forfeit all right, title, and interest in the Keweenaw Mountain Lodge premises.

As Keweenaw County resumed ownership of the Lodge, it became necessary for the Road Commission to advance the Board of Park Trustees $7,000 to fund reopening and operation of the resort for the 1968 season. Additionally, Keweenaw County government ended up having to fund the resolution of several liens that had been placed on the property—paying $10,939 to Gartner's

Furniture (to prevent Gartner's from repossessing the Lodge's dining room furniture) and $7,000 to Anderson Plumbing and Heating (in settlement of an $8,523 bill for work done on the Lodge's swimming pool).

The records for this period are not clear, however, it appears that as the Park Trustees resumed control of Lodge operations, their principal focus became one of doing whatever was necessary in order to (once again) sell the property. That said, among the more controversial operational issues which arose during the period related to the ending of the practice of spraying large amounts of the insecticide DDT around the park grounds and golf course. While there were safety and environmental concerns associated with use of the pesticide, the downside of not using DDT-based compounds was the seasonal return of uncontrolled—sometimes rampant—populations of black flies and mosquitoes.

A Mr. and Mrs. Mixon were brought on board to manage the resort for the 1968 season. Evidently, the following year, 1969, Dorothy Lodge—formerly the co-owner/co-operator of Copper Harbor's Lakeside Lodge—was hired as Manager. Given the continuation of difficult business conditions, however, Keweenaw Mountain Lodge ended up incurring losses in both years, <$10,648> in 1968 and <$3,233> in 1969.

Then, the Lodge was sold again. This time, on March 24, 1970, to a Michigan corporation, Project Developers, Inc. Project Developers was a legal entity principally comprised of two individuals, William T. Greig and Arthur C. Pontius. Keweenaw County agreed to finance the purchase with a five year land contract. Project Developers paid $15,000 to initiate the acquisition, promising to pay Keweenaw County a total contract purchase price of $160,000.

Art Pontius assumed the role of Keweenaw Mountain Lodge Manager effective with the start of the 1970 season. Similar to the Superior Development regime, Project Developers was woefully under capitalized and, subsequently, failed to make a required, January 1, 1971, $27,000 payment to Keweenaw County.

Ray Heikkinen, a resident of the Keweenaw Pines senior citizens housing complex in Ahmeek, recalled his time working as Head Greenskeeper for the Project Developers organization: "Art Pontius and his partner tried to run the Lodge in the winter—they tried to run it year round—but it just didn't work—there weren't any customers that time of year. They ran the operation through Christmas and into the New Year—and then they went belly-up. I remember that it was after the first of the New Year—Pontius and his partner just walked away—they didn't even bother to lock the front door—they just up and left. The County ended up with it back in their lap. I lost 16 days of pay—there was a bunch of us that got shortchanged—several other folks on the grounds crew and some of the kitchen help lost out, too. I talked with a lawyer about it, but because it was a land contract, there was nothing that any of us could do."

That spring—April 6, 1971—the Keweenaw County Board of Commissioners took action relative to the default, declaring the land contract between them and Project Developers void and forfeited. The Board authorized the initiation of legal action to recover possession of the Keweenaw Mountain Lodge property. Six months later—on October 7, 1971—Circuit Court Judge Stephen D. Condon found and ordered that Keweenaw County was the sole owner of the property.

THE MODERN ERA

As the Keweenaw Board of Park Trustees resumed operation of the Lodge for the 1971 season, they appointed Herman Koldewey as Manager. Koldewey had formerly worked at the Lodge during the "private ownership era" as Chef and maitre d'.

In becoming Manager, Koldewey joined a long list of accomplished and dedicated individuals who have served in the leadership role of Manager:

Clem Veale	1935–1963
Clarence Frederick	1964
Merle Richardson	1965–1967 (Private Ownership Era)
Mr. & Mrs. Mixon	1968
Nancy Lodge	1969
Art Pontius	1970 (Private Ownership Era)
Herman Koldewey	1971–1974
Jacqueline Jaaskelainen	1975 & 1976
Nancy Dragoo	1977–1989

Chuck Abe	1990–1995
Linda Lassila-Luusua	1996–1999
Bruce LeBlanc	2000
Darlene Bjorn	2001–2007
Cormac Ronan	2008–Present

Claire Turnquist, who served for nearly 30 years as Lodge Bookkeeper, filled-in several times as Acting Manager: Once following the mid-season, 1989, resignation of Nancy Dragoo; a second time—in 1995—when Chuck Abe, suffering from esophageal cancer, became too ill to work; and, a third time, following the August 1, 1999, resignation of Linda Lassila-Luusua.

Cormac Ronan became Manager on April 14, 2008; head of the modernized and expanded resort, he had previously spent 12 years at Michigan Technological University, including a stint at Portage Lake Golf Course. Attendant with Ronan becoming Manager, Darlene Bjorn, manager from 2001 through the 2007 season, took on the new challenge of Banquet and Conference Center Manager.

The job of Manager of the Keweenaw Mountain Lodge has never been an easy one. As retired KCRC Engineer Jim Heikkila observed: "It's a tough, pressure-packed, job. It is an intensely political position—in a very visible, public setting. You're just scrutinized so much in that job— with it being a County-owned and operated facility, there are some who are envious of the position—I've often thought that there is no one who could run the Lodge to the satisfaction of everyone."

Beyond the Manager position, the employment of individuals with many years of experience—with long association with the facility—has provided the Lodge with organizational stability, insuring continuity of operations.

Over the years there have been hundreds of employees who have spent countless hours—in some cases, years— "toiling in the trenches," making sure that customers were well served and that the Lodge is operated effectively.

One such employee was Sylvia Korpijarvi. In point of fact, if there were an award for greatest number of years of employee service at the Lodge, it might well belong to Sylvia. A resident of Fulton Location, Sylvia started working at the Lodge in 1973—and ended up spending the next 35 years employed there—working in the laundry, and in later years, cooking in the kitchen. With playfulness in her voice, Sylvia reflected on her many years of service: "Well, I never had to worry about running out of work—there was always plenty of dirty laundry—and if not, you could always count on someone being hungry."

A half dozen years following the resumption of County ownership, Lodge operations had stabilized and revenues were on the upswing—by the end of the 1977 season the facility had achieved a record level of sales—$270,014.

From the late 1970s—through the 1990s—dining was among the Lodge's principal sources of revenue. Jane Bjorn, who worked at the Lodge for 25 years, reminisced on the popularity of dining at the resort: "Between the Saturday night smorg (smorgasbord) and the Sunday morning buffet, it was amazing how many people would make a special trip to come and eat at the Lodge. Those of us who worked there—we used to have a pool as to how many people would show up for the Sunday buffet—each of us would throw a quarter into the pot. It was incredible—sometimes we'd get over 400 people on a Sunday—it was a real money maker."

The 1980s marked the beginning of a new stage in the development of the resort. The principal events which characterize this era include: 1) The 1984 Motel Addition; and, 2) The 2007 Lodge Expansion.

The 1984 Motel Addition:

The addition of a six-unit motel building to the Lodge's inventory of accommodations marked the first significant capital investment made at the resort following return of the facility to County ownership.

The motel addition, a 28 foot x 100 foot log-sided building, was constructed adjacent to what had been the swimming pool area.

Long-time KCRC Engineer, Jim Heikkila, recalled the Lodge swimming pool: "It was built back in the 1960s during the Superior Development of Indiana ownership—the swimming pool was set right on top of what would have been the #10 tee. I suspect that many years ago there must have been some blasting—some rock removal—some type of disturbance to the ground in that area; it might have occurred back in the 1930s when they were preparing the ground for the second nine holes of the golf course. What happened was that when they built the swimming pool, the contractor didn't compact the soil properly. There was frost heaving, the pool cracked crossways at the bottom and it wouldn't hold water. The original contractor refused to fix it and, when the County took back ownership of the Lodge, repairing the pool became something we tried to help with at the Road Commission."

Heikkila explained: "We could never find a way to fix it—part of the problem was that the crack ran right through the drain area. We tried—unsuccessfully—to repair it, but the foundation would shift and it would crack all over again. Eventually—right around the time the motel addition was under consideration—we had the pool filled-in with mine rock. We leveled the surface and paved it—that is how we solved the pool problem. Parking was always an issue up around the Lodge at that time, and if nothing else, it helped to resolve that issue."

With a bit of levity, Heikkila added, "The swimming pool—well, if anyone is looking for it—it's still right there—right under the surface of the motel parking lot."

The motel addition was designed by U.P Engineers and Architects. Construction began in May, 1984, with Arend Builders, Inc., of Eagle River erecting the structure. Dollar Bay's Valley Plumbing and Heating and Calumet's White Electrical Services served as the principal subcontractors for the project.

Designed to fill the need for shorter-term, day-to-day, visitor lodging, completion of the motel addition provided the Lodge with a total of 41 rental units, giving the facility the ability to accommodate over 100 guests each night.

The 2007 Lodge Expansion:

In 1988—four years after completion of the motel addition—discussions began relative to the possibility of converting the Lodge to year-round use. These conversations were based on the concept of winterizing the complex, marketing it as a winter-time cross country skiing resort.

A winterization feasibility study was prepared by Hitch, Inc.; it estimated a cost of $1.6 million to insulate and heat the Clubhouse, the 24 cottage units and the six-unit motel building. Additionally, the study contemplated a major upgrading of the Lodge's water, sewer and electrical systems.

After considerable analysis and discussion, the 1988 winterization proposal was shelved. Nevertheless, the proposition did have the longer-term effect of generating public discussion regarding the future development of the Lodge, helping to prompt creation of a county-wide recreation plan.

Financially, over the course of the late 1980s and early 1990s, Lodge revenues steadily improved, by 1998, increasing to $957,420. More importantly—the resort was consistently profitable—regularly generating positive cash flow averaging approximately $100,000 a year.

In 2003, discussions began anew relative to the possibility of expanding the Lodge. In contrast to earlier proposals, feasibility analyses focused not only on the idea of winterizing the resort, but on the possibility of expanding the Clubhouse, making it more of a community-centered facility.

In the spring of 2006, as part of the expansion study process, the Keweenaw County Board of Commissioners established a 10 member Parks and Recreation Commission, giving that entity responsibility for both oversight of the Lodge and management of the expansion project. Soon thereafter, U. P. Engineers and Architects was selected to provide the project with design services.

The design which was developed provided for the addition—at the rear of the Clubhouse—of a 7,000-square foot, banquet facility and conference center. The kitchen area was to be expanded, with a walkway being added to connect the Clubhouse to the conference center. The main lodge building—what younger individuals typically call the "Lodge," and what members of an older genre frequently refer to as the "Clubhouse"—was to be winterized, as was the six-unit motel building, and 13 of the 24 rental cottages. Improvements were to be made to transition water, sewer, electrical, and heating systems from seasonal to year-round use.

This broader concept—one of creating an expanded, year-round facility—received the go-ahead from Keweenaw County government.

Costing $3.3 million, the expansion and renovation project was principally financed by the combination of a $1.273 million USDA Rural Development loan and a $1.754 million U. S. Economic Development Administration grant. As a condition of the grant, Keweenaw County was required to make a good faith effort to operate the Lodge year-round, towards the objective of providing yearlong employment opportunities.

Following completion of competitive bidding, MJO Contracting, Inc., was selected as general contractor. As an entertaining historical detail, the President of MJO Contracting is Mick J. Oja—the grandson of Victor Oja, the individual who, 72 years earlier, served as KCRC's on-site Superintendent in charge of construction of the Clubhouse. Mick Oja thought back on the 2007 expansion project: "The most interesting part was when we did the demolition on the backside of the Lodge, preparing to attach it into the new addition—to look at the old log work—to see how, some 70 years before, they had built it and tied it all together—and to think that that was my grandfather's work…"

Construction began in November, 2006, and by late spring, 2007, the project was finished. That June, the U. P. Road Builders Association inaugurated use of the conference center. Later that summer—on July 21, 2007—a grand opening event was held to formally open the enlarged and renovated facility. Since completion of the expansion project, conference center rental and banquets—especially weddings—have accounted for a significant portion of the Lodge's revenue.

In the fall of 2007, the Keweenaw County Board of Commissioners, in what some considered a controversial maneuver, removed operational oversight of the Lodge from the Parks and Recreation Commission. Several members of the Parks and Recreation Commission resigned in protest of the Board's action. In spite of this, within a few months the Board of Commissioners—acting at its February 20, 2008, meeting—returned governance of the Lodge to the entity which had traditionally been in charge of the facility, the Keweenaw County Road Commission and its Board of Park Trustees.

The year 2008 marked the last year for operation of the Lodge's employee van-transportation system. Begun a few years following the shut-down of Shantytown, the silver and black colored vans were a common sight along US 41 as they ferried employees back and forth between the Lodge and points south, principally Mohawk and Ahmeek. Veteran employee Darlene Bjorn reminisced relative to the transit system: "The vans were always the source of some amazing stories—some of them incredibly humorous. Every trip there was the usual stop at the Phoenix Store for pop and ice cream—but then there was also the occasional stop along the way at a bar. Sometimes the vans carried employee's kids—and more than a few times, kids got left in the vans—one time they even took the backseat out of a van so that they could fit a motorcycle inside. The vans and the stories associated with them were always a never ending source of laughter and humor."

Bjorn reflected on her nearly 20 years of service at the Lodge: "You just can't imagine what it's been like to have been here all these years. The Lodge is a very special place. It's a historic building in an absolutely beautiful setting. But, what makes the Lodge special are the people. I've worked with an incredible number of wonderful people over the years. I've had the chance to meet people from all over the country—from just about every state—and nearly every one of them has been among the nicest people you'd ever want to meet. It's the people you meet—the people you get to know—their good times and their celebrations—that is what makes this such a special place."

Monday, December 28, 2009, saw the Lodge open for its first winter season since it was built 75 years earlier. Lodge Manager Cormac Ronan commented on the first month of winter operation: "We need more business—for that matter, right now—we could also use more snow. I was out on the golf course the other day and there was bare ground around the bases of most of the trees—something like that certainly is not typical for the Keweenaw in January. In terms of business, weekdays—Sunday through Thursday—have been slow—however, we're starting to get a fair number of people on the weekends. The

Lodge is beautiful in winter—my impression is that the people who have come up have had a wonderful time. It is going to take some time—it is critical that we get the word out that we're here and that we're open—however, everyone here at the Lodge is optimistic about winter operation. We are confident that the future is bright."

EPILOGUE

History can be complicated, and occasionally, messy. That is because it entails the telling of the stories of the past—the cataloging of names, dates, places and events—the reasons, assumptions and analyses as to why "what happened, happened."

Then there is a broader definition of history—the organized search for truth by examining the past. In that construct, history is not the objective. Rather, truth is—truth is the legitimate end.

Sometimes the best history involves debunking myths that have developed over long periods of time. Myths are fun—they make telling a story easier—they are memorable—certainly, they entertain us. Given a choice between a dull story as to how something happened, and an odd, curious or interesting one, we'll probably want to hear the latter.

Notwithstanding, history is strewn with myths—and that includes the history of the Keweenaw Mountain Lodge. And there is nothing wrong with that, unless someone would like to know what the truth is.

At least some of what has been told or written about the Lodge is not entirely true. And so, as we come to the end of the Keweenaw Mountain Lodge Story, here are three historical myths—fictional narratives and popular beliefs—that are not necessarily totally grounded in fact:

Myth #1—The Keweenaw Mountain Lodge was patterned after the Presidential retreat, Camp David:

It is not certain how this myth came to be, however, it has been published in or has otherwise been cited in numerous sources. By way of example, these include: 1) a historical article on the Lodge published in the September, 2006, issue of Marquette Monthly; 2) as supporting information in the Keweenaw County Planning and Development Commission's 2002 "Blueprint for Tomorrow— Land Use Plan;" and 3) as historical fact on the coppercountrytrail.org national byway tourist information website.

Camp David was started in 1935, when the WPA—trying to create a park out of worn-out agricultural land—began building the Catoctin Recreational Demonstration Project near Thurmont, Maryland. Three years later—in 1938—the facility, then known as Hi-Catoctin, was opened as a camp for federal government employees and their families. The facility consisted of several small cabins, a dining hall and a swimming pool.

After the start of World War II, the Hi-Catoctin site was selected as a secure retreat for President Franklin Roosevelt. Roosevelt visited the camp—operated by the Navy and renamed "U.S.S. Shangri La"—for the first time on July 18, 1942. A decade later, President Eisenhower changed the name of the retreat to Camp David, in honor of his grandson.

What the Keweenaw Mountain Lodge and Camp David have in common is that they are both retreats perched on heavily wooded hilltops. Both have a "golf course," although the Camp David "course" only amounts to a single hole. In contrast, and as one might expect for a Presidential retreat, there are a few things that Camp David has that the Lodge does not—a heated swimming pool, a sauna, two clay tennis courts, a two-lane bowling alley, a trout stream, a skeet-shooting and archery range, and a movie theatre.

Given the earlier timeline for the Lodge—beginning in 1933 as a CWA project— the Clubhouse being built in 1934 under the FERA program—the cottages being started as a WPA project in January, 1936—it is just not possible for Camp David to have been the prototype for the Keweenaw Park and Golf Course project.

Myth #2—The winter of 1933–1934 was one of the coldest on record:

This legend can be traced to the Lodge's official, one-page, historical handout, Keweenaw Mountain Lodge & Golf Course Story, written by retired KCRC Engineer, John W. Jackson.

Jackson wrote: "The winter of 1933–34 was one of the coldest on record with temperatures considerably below zero in January and February, but the huge pile of brush from the limbs of the trees being cut made good fires for the men to work near, and it was far from being a hardship."

Winters in the Keweenaw are never easy and Jackson, in writing the piece, probably relied upon his recollection of events. However, the winter of 1933–1934 was—in point of fact—relatively mild. Nevertheless, there was a winter during the early years of the Keweenaw Park and Golf Course project that was cold and bitter—and that was the winter of 1935–1936.

Readers will recall that January, 1936, marked the beginning of construction work on the "Cottages" project. At the time there would have been many men working outside. This may have been the "weather event" triggering Jackson's recollection.

According to Karl Bohnak's delightful abstract on U.P. weather, So Cold A Sky—Upper Michigan Weather Stories:

> "Relatively mild winters were the rule in Upper Michigan from the 1920s into the early 30s so residents were likely unprepared for the 'most severe and prolonged cold wave of many winters' that blew in during late January 1936. The arctic blast was preceded by 'a raging blizzard' on January 22 and 23, judged the worst in years.

> The storm brought travel to a virtual halt…strong winds blew the new snow into huge drifts, making travel nearly impossible. The snow finally let up, but the wind continued, transporting bitter arctic air which had been banked up to the northwest. While the blizzard raged in the U.P., Duluth reached 30 degrees below zero with a brutal northwesterly wind that gusted to 40 miles an hour.… An incredible 55 below zero was measured at a bridge linking the U.S. and Canada at International Falls.

> The cold wave of 1936 will be remembered for its harsh combination of wind and cold that persisted for nearly a month over a wide area of the Midwest and Great Lakes."

Obviously, in the big scheme of things, whether one winter is—or is not—colder than another is trivial and inconsequential. Nonetheless, this example—similar to the earlier "Camp David" myth—does illustrate that things are sometimes written without the authenticity of the underlying facts being verified.

Myth #3—"Potter's Folley:"

The "Potter's Folley" saga is listed here not because it didn't happen—but rather—because there is a deeper and more elaborate explanation as to how this popular parable became part of the telling of the history of the Lodge.

According to legend, at the start of the project, newspapers held the Keweenaw Park and Golf Course project up for ridicule, referring to it as "Potter's Folley." A variation on this narrative has people talking about the project as "Potter's Folley," remarking on the utter foolishness of spending taxpayer money for a "millionaire's playground."

The "Potter's Folley" tale is incredibly wide-spread—it appears in almost every modern-day article, publication or internet site touching on the background of the Keweenaw Mountain Lodge.

Here are a few things that we know:

- From the fall of 1933—when the Keweenaw Park and Golf Course project was conceived and first publicized—through the decade of the 1930s, every one of the Keweenaw's principal newspapers—the Calumet News, the Evening Copper Journal and the Daily Mining Gazette—supported the project. Each of the publications was positive in their reporting—each endorsed the project in their editorial sections. The Keweenaw Park and Golf Course project was never—not even once—referred to in these publications as "Potter's Folley."

- The sharpest criticism of the project seems to occur in a May, 1935, Detroit Free Press article written by E. L. Warner, Jr. Entitled, "U. P. Course Has Cost $8,000 Per Hole to Build," the newspaper reported that, "the course has cost a good-sized fortune…some have criticized it as a waste of money." The article continued, however, "…State officials justify it by pointing out the benefits to the area and explaining it is the only project which would fulfill the original CWA requirements and provide enough jobs." The adage "Potter's Folley" never appears in the article.

- The first time the epithet "Potter's Folley" appears in print is 1941. In a Sunday, September 7, 1941, Chicago Tribune article entitled "Now Copper Country Cops Tourist Cash," travel writer Frederic Babcock chronicled the development of the Keweenaw Park project, writing that at the beginning of the project, people talked derisively about it, referring to it as "Potter's Field," and "Potter's Folley."

In summary, the term "Potter's Folley" never appeared in print prior to 1941. After that date, there is rarely an article written which doesn't use the epithet. Clearly, John W. Jackson was on target when he wrote in his one-page Keweenaw Mountain Lodge & Golf Course Story, "Even the city newspaper picked it up later and called it Potter's Folley."

This begs the question, did anyone actually refer to the project as "Potter's Folley?" The answer is, yes—almost certainly.

The project did, after all, entail the building of a golf course in the northern reaches of a county where hardly anyone golfed. In that atmosphere, the Keweenaw Park and Golf Course project—much like any other government-sponsored work relief program—would have been the subject of criticism, including the occasional derisive comment. Still, cracks about "Potter's Folley," were likely the exception, not the rule—the aphorism was probably never used to the extent that contemporary articles seem to imply.

Stan Martin, in recalling the original construction of the Lodge, reflected on the "Potter's Folley" legend: "There was some grousing when the golf course and Clubhouse were being built, but not as much as people have been led to believe. There was some ribbing of Ocha Potter—it was mostly good natured and done in fun—but, in actuality, there wasn't all that much that was even said about the project."

Martin continued, "The thing is, before anyone knew it, the golf course was done and the Clubhouse was up. And once that happened, no one complained about it any more—it was done—it was over. What are you going to do about it then? No one mentioned it any more. In terms of the project being controversial—in terms of it being "Potter's Folley"—well, that really didn't come up until considerably later—probably in the early 1940s, coinciding with that (Chicago Tribune) newspaper article. And then it was repeated over and over and over again, and before anyone knew it, it became accepted as gospel."

And the validity of the "millionaire's playground" wisecrack? It is certainly possible that the statement was made, especially considering that it must have seemed exotic—in the middle of the worst economic depression ever faced by the nation—for the federal government to have been funding the construction of a golf course.

However, to place the Keweenaw Park project into historical perspective, it was one of hundreds of golf courses that were built in the 1930s under the auspices of the CCC, CWA, FERA and WPA programs. Most of these depression-era "work relief" golf courses were built as municipal projects, although some were constructed for county, state, or federal entities.

Counted among these golf courses were many located in the mid-west: Phillips Park Golf Course, Aurora, IL; Keller Park Golf Course, St. Paul, MN; Milham Park Municipal Golf Course, Kalamazoo, MI; Ohio State University Golf Course, Columbus, OH; and, Whitnall Golf Course, Hales Corners, Milwaukee, WI. A few of the "WPA courses" even became famous—among them the magnificent Black Course at Bethpage State Park on Long Island, New York—host of the 2002 and 2009 U. S. Open National Golf Championships.

Harry Hopkins, in his 1936 treatise on federal work relief programs, said, "Long after the workers of CWA are dead and gone and these hard times are forgotten, their effort will be remembered by permanent useful works in every county in every state." The passage of time has demonstrated that Hopkins, far from creating another myth, had voiced the true promise of the New Deal's work relief programs. Indeed, the Keweenaw Mountain Lodge stands as evidence that there was a time in our past when people chose to fight anguish and despair by building for the future.

Acknowledgments

Many individuals and organizations have helped make the telling of this story possible.

For assistance with research and photographs, thanks to: Dick Rupley; Julie Carlson-Keweenaw County Clerk & Register of Deeds; Ginny Jamison-Keweenaw County Historical Society; Gregg Patrick, Steve DeFour, Lori Reilly and Ken Rowe-Keweenaw County Road Commission; Cormac Ronan, Darlene Bjorn and Michele Olson-Keweenaw Mountain Lodge; Erik Nordberg and Julie Blair-Michigan Tech Archives and Copper Country Historical Collections; Rosemary Michelin-John M. Longyear Research Library, Marquette County Historical Society; and Lori Hauswirth-Western Upper Peninsula Planning and Development Region.

For opening doors, sharing memories and providing insights, thanks to: Mary Billings, Darlene Bjorn, Jane Bjorn, Jim Boggio, Bob Carlton, Bill Clark, Bob & Judy Davis, Jacquie Jaaskelainen, Jim Heikkila, Ray Heikkinen, Rich Jamsen, Sylvia Korpijarvi, Stan Martin, Mick Oja, Carol Patrick, Gregg Patrick, Hank Pellikka, Walter Riistola, Frank Stubenrauch, Claire Turnquist, Jerry Vairus, Joe Waananen, Clyde & Lloyd Wescoat, and Don Zappa.

Photo Credits

Paul LaVanway collection, William (Bill) Clark, Keweenaw Country Road Commission, Keweenaw County Historical Society and Michigan Technological University Copper Country Archives and Historical Collections.

www.ingramcontent.com/pod-product-compliance
Lightning Source LLC
Chambersburg PA
CBHW042246300426
44110CB00031B/160